INSIDE DINOSAURS

AND OTHER

PREHISTORIC CREATURES

INSIDE DINOSAURS
AND OTHER
PREHISTORIC CREATURES

Illustrated by Ted Dewan
Written by Steve Parker

DORLING KINDERSLEY
London • New York • Stuttgart

DK

A Dorling Kindersley Book

Project Editor   Laura Buller
Art Editors   Sarah Ponder and Diane Clouting
Production   Susannah Straughan
Consultant   William Lindsay
Managing Editor   Helen Parker
Managing Art Editor   Peter Bailey

First published in Great Britain in 1993 by
Dorling Kindersley Limited, 9 Henrietta Street,
London WC2E 8PS

A CIP catalogue record for this book
is available from the British Library

ISBN 0 7513 5055 9

Reproduced in Essex by Dot Gradations

Printed in Italy by A. Mondadori Editore, Verona

To Gramps - the greatest dinosaur in 64 million years - T.D.

*To the memory of my father, Ron,
who would have been proud - but puzzled! - S.P.*

CONTENTS

INTRODUCTION   6

READING THE BONES   8
IGUANODON

TEETH AND JAWS   10
*TYRANNOSAURUS, HETERODONTOSAURUS,
AND RHOETOSAURUS*

NECK AND NECK   12
*DIPLODOCUS, CERATOSAURUS, AND
MAMENCHISAURUS*

ON ALL FOURS   14
*DIPLODOCUS AND
ANCHISAURUS*

TAIL-ENDERS   16
*EUOPLOCEPHALUS, DIPLODOCUS,
PACHYCEPHALOSAURUS, AND STEGOSAURUS*

UP AND RUNNING   18
*PACHYCEPHALOSAURUS, STRUTHIOMIMUS,
AND COMPSOGNATHUS*

SLASH AND GNASH 20
DEINONYCHUS AND BARYONYX

ARMOURED AND DANGEROUS 22
HYLAEOSAURUS AND TRICERATOPS

HOLES IN THE HEAD 24
PARASAUROLOPHUS, CORYTHOSAURUS, AND EDMONTOSAURUS

BRAINS AND BODIES 26
STEGOSAURUS AND STENONYCHOSAURUS

SENSITIVE DINOSAURS 28
CAMARASAURUS, STRUTHIOMIMUS, AND CORYTHOSAURUS

DINOSAUR DIGESTION 30
BRACHIOSAURUS AND ALLOSAURUS

BREATHING AND BLOOD 32
APATOSAURUS

A HEATED DEBATE 34
SPINOSAURUS AND STEGOSAURUS

EGGS AND BABIES 36
PROTOCERATOPS

PREHISTORIC OCEANS 38
PLESIOSAURUS, ICHTHYOSAURUS, AND ARCHELON

PREHISTORIC SKIES 40
PTERANODON AND PTERODAUSTRO

CREEPY-CRAWLIES 42
GIANT CENTIPEDE, COCKROACH, AND DRAGONFLY

FUR AND FEATHER 44
ARCHAEOPTERYX AND PROBELESODON

SLIDE TO EXTINCTION 46

INDEX 48

Tools to expose fossils

Site is photographed

Fossil wrapped in a protective layer of plaster

IN THE FIELD
Where do you find a dinosaur? Fossils are found only in sedimentary rocks, laid down in layers on the beds of rivers, lakes, and seas, or in deserts. Rock surrounding the find is carefully cleaned away, while scientists take photos, and make sketches and notes. Some fossils are wrapped in protective jackets.

Number linked to maps of site

INTRODUCTION

INSIDE A DINOSAUR? You're kidding! No one ever saw a living, breathing dinosaur – not even a caveperson, since the last dinos died more than 60 million years before the first humans appeared. All that is left of these creatures are bones, teeth, horns, and claws, which turned to stone and formed fossils.

But fossils are valuable clues. For instance, we know from today's animals that flat-topped teeth are for chewing tough plant food. Long, pointy teeth are designed to kill. Straight away, just one fossil tooth can identify its owner as a plant-eater or hunter. Weird and wonderful fossils of dinosaur eggs, last dinners, and dino-droppings give further glimpses of their living habits. The remains of other animals and plants found with the fossils, and the rocks surrounding them, tell us about the place a dinosaur called home. Of course, there is still plenty of guesswork. Soft parts, such as brains, hearts, and skin, rarely fossilized. But a little detective work can bring a dino back to life…well, almost.

Our previous book, *Inside the Whale and other Animals*, took creatures apart from the outside in. This book puts animals back together, from the inside out. The dinosaurs and other featured creatures that stalked, swam, flew, ran, and lumbered over the planet will give you a peek into the strange and ferocious world that was prehistoric Earth.

Ted Dewan

Steve Parker

BACK TO THE LAB
A huge dinosaur fossil is solid rock – so it's very heavy. It may be a long, hard road from a remote fossil site to the comfort of the workshop.

CHECK IN
The fossils are carefully unwrapped and checked. All finds are catalogued and numbered. Your fossil might make headlines, so you'd better not lose it!

Rock dissolves, but fossils are not damaged

Fossils lowered into vat of acid

EXTRACTING THE FOSSILS
Experts use various methods to clear away the rock around the fossil, including acid baths.

Only newsworthy fossils get instant attention – others go to the vaults.

FILL IN THE BLANKS
Few fossil skeletons are
complete or in perfect
condition. It takes a
good knowledge of bones,
from the living and long-
gone, to fill in the
missing parts.

*Missing
bones can be
cast from
moulds of
existing bones*

TAKING SHAPE
Gradually the bones are pieced together
on a framework. They are often moulded
fibreglass copies, which are lighter
than solid-rock fossils. It's also
less shattering if they
fall and break!

*Drawings
made of
each fossil*

*Design
decisions
made here*

*Rhino
body plan
studied for
similarities*

*Fossilized
impressions
show what
skin was like*

FROM RHINO TO DINO
To understand a peculiar body
feature, such as a horn, look
for parallels among
animals alive today.
Studying the
similarities may shed
light on the
horn's use.

*Protective
jacket
removed*

*Liquid plastic
brushed on to
strengthen fossil*

*Leftover
bones*

*Markings on
bone show where
to attach muscles*

Fossil claws

BACK TO LIFE
And here it is –
Triceratops, one of
the last and best known of the
dinosaurs. It dwelled 70 million years
ago, in what we now call North America.
So now that you've seen how to find and
reconstruct a dinosaur, on with the book…

*More
muscles*

READING THE BONES

MOST OF WHAT WE THINK WE KNOW about dinosaurs comes from the study of their preserved remains: chiefly bones, teeth, horns, and claws. These provide several clues. From just a few fossil bones, for example you can make a good stab at the creature's overall size. The fossil's shape gives even more clues. If you have a working knowledge of similar animal skeletons, living and extinct, you can assign a bone to a body part by its shape alone. Surface details lead to other discoveries. Ridges, rough or smooth patches, holes, and grooves indicate the positions of muscle and tendon attachments, nerves, and blood vessels. Gradually, the pieces of the jigsaw fit together and produce something more: a picture of the dinosaur's behaviour and way of life.

CRESTS AND RIDGES
Lumps, crests, and ridges on bones like the bump on this thigh bone imply muscle attachments – especially if the surface is roughened and pitted in texture. This was where the muscle's tendon grew into and anchored on the bone, for strength and pulling power. The bumps and flanges provided extra surface area, and angled the bone's surface so that the muscle could pull it more efficiently.

IGUANODON
This ten-metre-long beast from 120 million years ago was one of the first dinosaurs to be officially named and described – on the evidence of teeth alone. English doctor and fossil-hunter Gideon Mantell, with his wife Mary Ann, found the teeth in about 1821. Noting their similarity to those of an iguana, lizard, he described the owner of the teeth in 1825 as *Iguanodon* ("iguana tooth").

MISSING PIECES
If you had a nearly-finished jigsaw, you could probably guess what the missing pieces looked like. A fossil skeleton is rarely complete. So in the same way, missing parts are reconstructed, or borrowed from other, similar dinosaurs. A missing tail vertebra (backbone), for example, could be mocked up following a standard tapering pattern.

Large tail vertebra

Medium tail vertebra

Small tail vertebra

Femur (thigh bone)

Bump on femur for tendon attachment

Bird-like hip bone

Phalanges (toe bones)

Metatarsal bone from foot

BIG FOOT, OR BIG HAND?
Some dinosaurs have been reconstructed with their forelimbs and hindlimbs the wrong way round. The size of *Iguanodon*'s hip bones, compared to its shoulders, implies that the dinosaur's legs were larger than its arms. Long, strong toe bones show that the creature may have walked on two sets of tippy-toes.

Fibula (calf bone)

Tibia (shin bone)

Strong framework for solid-rock fossils

Bony rods
to stiffen
spine

FILLING THE GAP
The vertebrae follow a shallow curve along
the back, indicating the animal's habitual
posture. The numbers should match up –
a pair of ribs for every vertebra
with rib joints.

*Relatively large
skull*

*Long
snout*

*Terminal
phalanx of
first digit
(thumb bone)…*

…fits here

*Vertebrae in
curved line
suggest flexible
neck*

*Angle of ribs
with vertebrae
shows size of
chest*

*Humerus
(upper arm
bone)*

*Skeleton
of emu*

*Radius (forearm
bone)*

*Ulna (forearm
bone)*

NOSE OR THUMB?
In an early reconstruction of
Iguanodon, a spiky bone was
placed on its nose, like a rhino's
horn. Yet it seemed to have no
sensible function here, being too
small for a weapon or sign of
status. There were also too many
spikes for the number of
skeletons found, yet no bones for
the thumb. The spike fitted better
on the thumb, where it could be
used as a leaf-stripper, and a
jabbing defensive weapon.

UPS AND DOWNS
Iguanodon is often shown
standing upright on its back
legs. Its middle three fingers,
however, were broad and
capped with tough hooves. This
indicates that it walked or
rested down on all fours for
some of the time.

IGGY'S THE ONE
If you wanted to learn about
studying dinosaur fossils,
Iguanodon would be a good
subject. Hundreds of its
skeletons, some amazingly
complete, have been unearthed
from Germany, Belgium, and
England. The sites themselves
yield more clues. For example,
bones from many individuals
have been found together,
suggesting this dinosaur
lived in herds.

MODERN COMPARISONS
We can watch today's animals
at work and play, study their
skeletons to relate form to
function, and then draw similarities to
extinct animals such as dinosaurs. This
modern bird, the Australian emu, is one
inspiration for *Iguanodon*'s two-legged
pose and vertebral curvature.

TEETH AND JAWS

BEING TRAPPED IN THE TEETH of *Tyrannosaurus* was no joke. Rows of daggers longer than your hand, with edges serrated like steak knives, biting with crushing force, could chop through your arm in an instant. Dinosaur teeth, being very hard, make excellent fossils. Their sizes, shapes, and positions in the jaws provide vital clues to favourite foods. They show if a dinosaur was a meat-slicing carnivore or a plant-crushing herbivore.

Capiti-mandibularis (jaw-closing) muscle

Skull

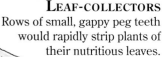

LEAF-COLLECTORS
Rows of small, gappy peg teeth would rapidly strip plants of their nutritious leaves.

Upper jaw

Lower jaw

Jaw joint

RAKING IT IN
Rows of small, slim, blunt teeth with gaps between them were ideal for raking leaves and buds from trees, and pulling fruits and seeds from plants.

DOWN UNDER
Rhoetosaurus was a medium-sized herbivore whose remains were found near Brisbane, Australia, in 1924. It lived during the Jurassic Period, around 200-150 million years ago. The fossils were one of the first major dinosaur discoveries "down under".

BATTERY-TOOTHED DUCKBILL
Anatosaurus was a 12-metre-long hadrosaur or "duckbilled" dinosaur. Behind its long, horn-covered beak were rows of strong cheek teeth, able to grind hard twigs and pine cones to a mulch.

Upper jaw

Young growing teeth

Teeth in use

Dentine tooth body

Enamel plate

Grinding surfaces wear at an angle

Vend-o-dent

BITING BILL
The beak was composed of tough, strong-edged horn that grew continuously – ideal for stripping vegetation.

TEAMS OF TEETH
New batches of hadrosaur teeth grew continuously, from the outside of the upper jaw and inside of the lower jaw. The plates of enamel wore more slowly than the rest of the tooth, giving a ridged surface for up-and-down chewing motions.

WHAT A MOUTHFUL
Anatosaurus and the other hadrosaurs had hundreds of teeth. Along the side of each jaw was a battery of up to 60 groups of teeth, five or six teeth in a group. They would grind and rub past each other, crushing the plants.

SCAVENGING BY SMELL?
When a large dinosaur died, it would rot and smell. *Tyrannosaurus* may have been a scavenger as well as a hunter. It probably found its next meal by following the scent of rotting meat.

Openings in skull bone

Jaw-closing muscles

DINOSAUR SUPER STRENGTH
The muscles and joints in *Tyrannosaurus*' jaw and neck were very strong. Perhaps the king reptile charged prey like a battering ram, absorbing the shock of impact with its heavy bones and joints. Its teeth would clamp onto the victim, and its strong neck would twist and jerk to rip out a chunk of flesh.

JAWS OF DEATH
The supreme carnivore *Tyrannosaurus* possessed the most fearsome teeth in the dinosaur world. A lunge, a clamping bite, a tug and a tear, and its prey was dead meat.

BABY TEETH
Throughout its life, new teeth were continually growing from tiny beginnings in the sockets inside *Tyrannosaurus*' jawbone. So the dinosaur was sure of a set of 50 or so stabbing, slicing weapons.

Neckbones were thick and strong to support the large head

TYRANNOSAURUS
Weighing in at seven tonnes, *Tyrannosaurus* would have been heavier than two of today's bull elephants. At more than five metres high, it was also taller than most giraffes, and twice as long as a fully grown great white shark.

TEETH FOR ALL SEASONS
Heterodontosaurus, which means "mixed-tooth reptile", had teeth of different shapes, more like a mammal such as you than a typical reptile. Sharp teeth at the front snipped and cut. Pointed teeth just behind speared and tore. Wide, flat back teeth chewed and ground.

Heterodontosaurus *was as tall as a labrador dog, and just over a metre long.*

Flat, crushing back teeth

Chiselling front teeth

Pointed teeth for spearing

EATING BETWEEN MEALS
The food of plant-eating dinosaurs such as *Heterodontosaurus* and *Anatosaurus* was probably tough and not very nourishing. Plant-eaters would have to feed and munch for most of the day to get enough nutrition. The rich flesh food of a meat-eater was easier to chew and digest, and it yielded more dietary goodness. The result: lazy large carnivores and ever-eating herbivores.

Strangely tiny arm

Two clawed fingers on hand

NECK AND NECK

THE FAMOUS SWAN'S NECK has nothing on the immensely long, snaking necks of some dinosaurs. Members of the sauropod group, such as *Diplodocus* and *Apatosaurus*, were the champion stretched-necks. But why did the process of evolution come up with such a bizarre body plan? Standing on one spot, *Diplodocus* could sweep its head in an arc almost 20 metres across, saving energy while stripping the surrounding low vegetation of nourishment. That done, it could stretch up and reach plant food five or six metres above the ground, all without shifting its immense bulk. After craning its neck to look and sniff for predators and other dangers, the giant dinosaur would lumber on to the next vegetable patch.

Nostril

A ROW OF PENCILS
Diplodocus had two arcs of pencil-like teeth at the front of its jaws, but its jaw muscles were weak. This dinosaur probably just raked off its leafy food and swallowed it straight away.

SMALL HEAD
The eyes and nostrils are set to the rear and top of *Diplodocus'* tiny head. At one time, people believed these types of dinosaur lived in deep lakes, and the long neck was a snorkel or underwater breathing tube.

FLEXI-NECK
Sets of muscles ran alongside the prongs and flanges of the spinal bones (vertebrae) in the neck. The muscles contracted in teams to pull the neck to one side, or twist it so the dinosaur could look to the side.

The skull was large for the body

BUMP ON THE HEAD
The rhino-like nose lump had a core of bone. Its function is not clear. Possibly it was a sign of maturity and of status when mating.

Tiny head

Flexible part of neck

Neck muscles bulge at rear of skull

Nostril

Stiffer part of neck

There were about six neck vertebrae

NO ESCAPE
As in other carnosaurs, the teeth curve backward into the mouth, to prevent the escape of struggling prey.

Muscles alongside chest vertebrae

SHORT AND STRONG
Ceratosaurus had a short but relatively powerful and flexible neck. It may have swung its head to snap at victims, and tug off pieces of flesh by a twisting and sawing motion.

CARNIVORE COUSINS
The "horned reptile" *Ceratosaurus* gets its name from the bump on its nose. It was some six metres long and stood two-and-a-half metres high. Fossils indicate that it was a meat-eating relative of the better-known *Allosaurus*. It stalked western North America during the late Jurassic Period, about 150 million years ago.

Rib

Neck vertebra

Hollowed-out areas
to save weight

Joint between
neck vertebrae

DIPLODOCUS

Diplodocus was one of the longest
dinosaurs of all time. Its skull and 100 or so
vertebrae stretched 27 metres, although half of this was the thin, whippy tail that ends four
pages away. This sauropod lumbered across western North America 140 million years ago.

Neck muscle attached
to upright flange on
vertebra

Oesophagus

Trachea

TWIN TUBES

In every dinosaur, just as in other reptiles,
and birds and mammals, the neck contains
two flexible tubes. These are the
oesophagus (gullet) for swallowed food,
and the trachea (windpipe) for breathed air.

Elastic ligaments along the
tops of the vertebrae helped
to hold up the head

Spinal
cord

Neck muscle
anchored to side
wing of vertebra

Dorsal flange or
projection of neck

Brain

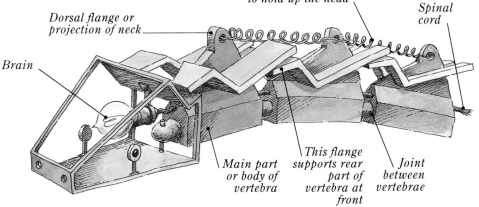

Main part
or body of
vertebra

This flange
supports rear
part of
vertebra at
front

Joint
between
vertebrae

HOW THE NECK WORKED

This mechanical neck shows the main
dinosaur features. Each vertebra of the
spine has bony projections called
processes or flanges on the top and sides,
to which the muscles are attached. Between
these, and above the main part, or body, of
each vertebra is a hole. The holes line up
and form a tunnel that protects the spinal
cord, the main bundle of nerves linking the
brain to the body. Long, stretchy ligaments
linked the vertebrae, to help stabilize the
neck and support the head.

The total length of Mamenchisaurus *from
head to tail tip was about 22 metres.*

THE LONGEST NECK

A sauropod from eastern Asia, *Mamenchisaurus*, has the longest of all
dinosaur necks – 11 metres, about half of the beast's total body length.
Reconstructions of the neck from the fossils of several individuals
show bendy portions near the head and shoulders, with a
relatively stiff centre section.

Bulky tail base
narrowed to a
whiplash tip

Flexible
part of
neck

Elephant-
like feet

ON ALL FOURS

IF YOU ARE AN AVERAGE TEN-YEAR-OLD (and who isn't, at heart?), each of your feet supports about 15 kilograms. Each of *Diplodocus'* feet carried two hundred times as much weight! But the dinosaur was rock steady on them, since its head and neck (on the previous two pages) counterbalanced its tail (on the next three pages).

Thoraco-scapular muscle

Scapula (shoulder blade)

Cervical (neck) vertebra

Posterior intervertebral joint

Anterior intervertebral joint

Creased skin over elbow joint

ANCHISAURUS

Anchisaurus ("close reptile") was about two-and-a-half metres long, but only as tall as a sheep. It was a prosauropod, an early Jurassic forerunner of the huge sauropods, such as *Diplodocus*, *Brachiosaurus,* and *Apatosaurus.*

DISPUTED DIET
Experts have proposed various diets for *Anchisaurus*. It probably ate anything it could grab with its blunt, small teeth.

SMALL WONDER
With small, slim bones, *Anchisaurus* was probably of a light build and relatively agile, able to scramble away from its enemies. It lived early in the Age of Dinosaurs, 195 million years ago.

Scapulo-humeralis muscle

Scapulo-deltoideus muscle

Elbow joint

Extensor digitorum muscles

Scapulo-humeralis muscle

Caudi-femoralis muscle

Ilio-tibialis muscle

Stomach

Heart *Lung*

Scapulo-deltoideus muscle

ON ALL TWOS?
Anchisaurus had the same basic muscles and bones as *Diplodocus*. However, its front legs were less developed than the back ones, so it may have moved only on the back pair for some of the time.

Dorsal processes (neural spines) of vertebrae

Coccygeal-ilialis muscle

Ilio-tibialis muscle

Ilium (hip bone)

BALANCED BEAMS

Think of a *Diplodocus* as a cantilever-type suspension bridge. The lengthy structure is balanced half-and-half over two huge pairs of supporting columns (legs), which bear the full weight. From the thick main cables (spinal vertebrae) hang thinner vertical cables (ribs). These steady the heavy roadway (guts, heart, and lungs).

Caudi-femoralis muscle

Sixth rib

Lungs

MAN-SIZED RIBS

The biggest of *Diplodocus'* 20 trunk ribs was longer than an adult human. The ribs arched down from attachments on the spine to enclose and protect the lungs, heart, and intestines.

Left pubic bone

Right pubic bone

Knee joints

Femoralis-tarsus muscle

STRAIGHT AHEAD

The humero-ulnaris muscle joins the upper end of the humerus (upper-arm bone) with the upper end of the ulna (forearm bone). As the muscle shortens, it straightens the elbow joint, thrusting the front end of the dinosaur forward. In your arm, this muscle is known as the triceps.

Tendon of ilio-tibialis muscle

Fibula (calf bone)

Tibia (shin bone)

FULL SUPPORT GIRDLES

Four-legged animals like dinosaurs have two girdles, or sets of bones and muscles. The pectoral girdle, better known as the shoulders, connects the upper spine and rib cage to the front limbs. The pelvic girdle, or hips, links the lower spine to the rear limbs. (Muscle names are explained on p.18.)

WRIST AND ANKLE BANDS

Straps of tough, elastic ligaments ran around each wrist and ankle. They kept the muscles and tendons near to the bones, as the feet flexed to and fro.

Tarsals (ankle bones)

BIGFOOT

Vastly wide feet with splayed toes helped to spread *Diplodocus'* weight.

15

TAIL-ENDERS

DINOSAUR TAILS DID MORE than just trail along behind their owners. They were long whips, spiky maces, muscle anchors, adjustable counterweights, steering rudders, or, in the case of *Euoplocephalus*, heavy clubs capable of knocking a predator for six. The dinosaurs shown here were all plant-eaters. They lacked the large, sharp teeth and claws of the carnivores, which doubled as both feeding utensils and defensive weapons. Self-defence gadgets evolved at the other end of their body.

SHARP, SPIKY REAR-SPEARS
Stegosaurus (p.26) had two pointy pairs of bone-cored tail spikes. Together, they formed a fierce, mace-like weapon, which was swung from side to side to puncture a predator.

Larger spike was more than 60 cm long

Base embedded in skin

AN ARRAY OF ARMOUR
Euoplocephalus sported a formidable array of spikes, spines, shields, and plates. It must have been an awkward mouthful for its tyrannosaur predators. As you might expect from a dinosaur whose name means "true plated head", even the eyelids are armoured.

Paired large dorsal spines

Shoulder spear

Neck shield

Shoulder nodule

Temple spike

Bony eyelid plate

BEAK AND TEETH
With a broad, toothless beak at the front of its jaws and small, weak cheek teeth, *Euoplocephalus* probably fed on soft, easy-to-chew vegetation.

Cheek spine

Bony lumps on forearm

Dorsal intervertebral muscles

Dorsal process

Transverse intervertebral muscles

Transverse (side) process

Intervertebral joint

Tough, leathery skin

Elbow joint

Ilio-tibialis muscles

Wrist joint

Clawed front foot

MISTER WHIPPY
The vertebrae midway along *Diplodocus*' tail had sideways and dorsal (upper) processes to anchor muscles. The joints between the vertebrae were relatively flexible, so *Diplodocus* could whip the tip of its tail at will, wielding it as an effective lash. Perhaps it cracked its tail like a ringmaster, frightening away enemies with the sound.

Dorsal and transverse processes anchor muscles

Tapering vertebrae

EUOPLOCEPHALUS

This medium-sized ankylosaur was about the size of a school minibus: six metres long, just taller than an adult, and two tonnes in weight. As dinosaurs go, it is fairly well known, from 80 million-year-old fossils unearthed in Alberta, western Canada.

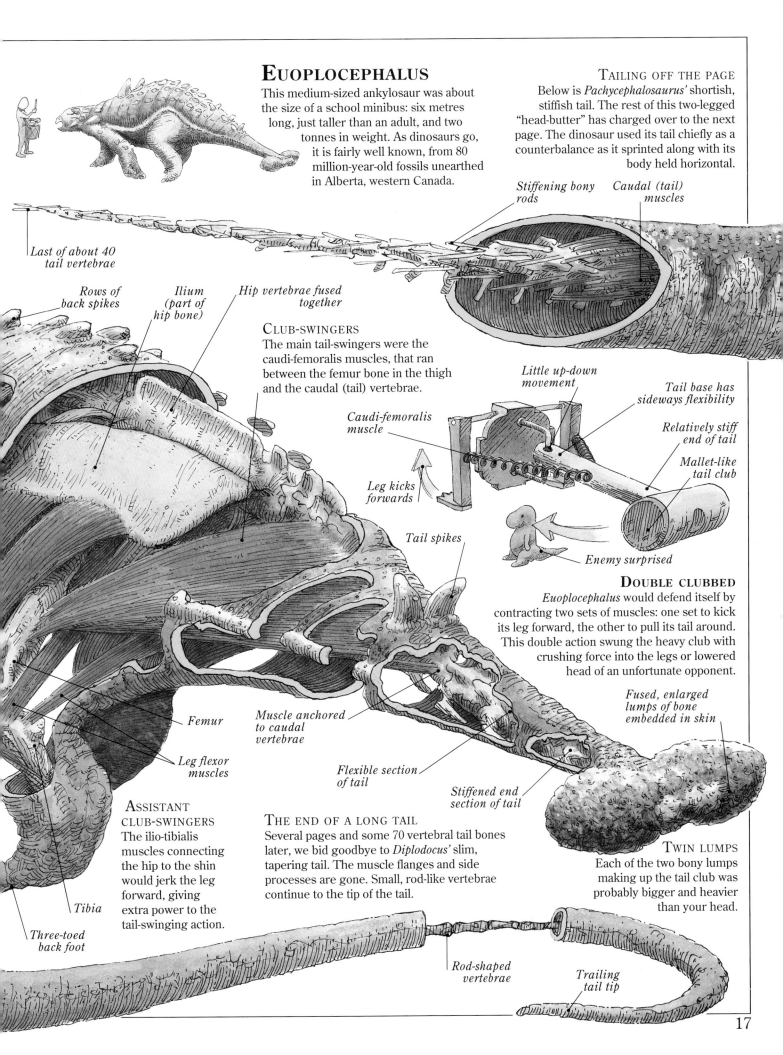

TAILING OFF THE PAGE
Below is *Pachycephalosaurus'* shortish, stiffish tail. The rest of this two-legged "head-butter" has charged over to the next page. The dinosaur used its tail chiefly as a counterbalance as it sprinted along with its body held horizontal.

Stiffening bony rods

Caudal (tail) muscles

Last of about 40 tail vertebrae

Rows of back spikes

Ilium (part of hip bone)

Hip vertebrae fused together

CLUB-SWINGERS
The main tail-swingers were the caudi-femoralis muscles, that ran between the femur bone in the thigh and the caudal (tail) vertebrae.

Caudi-femoralis muscle

Little up-down movement

Tail base has sideways flexibility

Relatively stiff end of tail

Mallet-like tail club

Leg kicks forwards

Tail spikes

Enemy surprised

DOUBLE CLUBBED
Euoplocephalus would defend itself by contracting two sets of muscles: one set to kick its leg forward, the other to pull its tail around. This double action swung the heavy club with crushing force into the legs or lowered head of an unfortunate opponent.

Femur

Muscle anchored to caudal vertebrae

Fused, enlarged lumps of bone embedded in skin

Leg flexor muscles

Flexible section of tail

Stiffened end section of tail

ASSISTANT CLUB-SWINGERS
The ilio-tibialis muscles connecting the hip to the shin would jerk the leg forward, giving extra power to the tail-swinging action.

THE END OF A LONG TAIL
Several pages and some 70 vertebral tail bones later, we bid goodbye to *Diplodocus'* slim, tapering tail. The muscle flanges and side processes are gone. Small, rod-like vertebrae continue to the tip of the tail.

TWIN LUMPS
Each of the two bony lumps making up the tail club was probably bigger and heavier than your head.

Tibia

Three-toed back foot

Rod-shaped vertebrae

Trailing tail tip

17

UP AND RUNNING

HEAD DOWN, NECK STRAIGHT OUT IN FRONT, tail stiff behind, body well balanced over muscular back legs, *Pachycephalosaurus* prepares to charge at a rival in the mating game. Many two-legged dinosaurs were slim and long-limbed, a sure sign of speed all those millions of years ago, just as it is in today's racehorses and ostriches.

ROD-RIGID
Small bony rods linked the vertebrae of the backbone and helped to stiffen it in the back and hip area.

Hip joint

Rear ribs

Ilium (main part of hip bone)

IN THE PINK
The hip muscles of *Pachycephalosaurus* are colour-coded for clarity. The dark pink ones (extensors) pull the upper leg back. The orange ones (flexors) pull it forward.

Muscle connecting tail to femur (thigh bone)

Muscles connecting ischium (hip bone) to femur (thigh bone)

Muscle connecting tail to tibia (shin)

Right femur (thigh bone)

Right knee joint

KNEES UP
The ilio-tibialis muscle joins the ilial part of the hip bone to the shin, or tibia, to raise the knee.

Muscles connecting tibia (shin) to tarsus (ankle)

Stiffened tail tip

Tail

Head and neck

Rear leg under body's centre of gravity

Shaft of tibia (shin bone)

Skin covers ankle

BALANCING THE BODY
Some older reconstructions of two-legged dinosaurs show them running in an upright position, chest and neck vertical. This would have been very tiring! It is more likely that they tipped head and neck forward so that the body's weight was centred over the rear legs. At rest, the body would tilt more upright, so the dinosaur could scan and sniff for danger.

MUSCLES
Dinosaurs, like humans, had several hundred body muscles. One common system for identifying them is to combine the names of the bones to which they are attached at each end. For example, the tibialis-tarsus pulls on the tibia (shin) and tarsus (ankle), to tip the toes down.

First toe is a short "spur"

Three clawed toes

Metatarsals (foot bones)

Metatarsal bones (main part of foot) under skin

Knuckles (toe joints)

Phalanges (toe bones)

THIRD LEVER
Compared to a plodder such as *Diplodocus*, the foot bones of *Pachycephalosaurus* are long and slim. Like the thigh and shin, the foot was a lever to increase running efficiency.

PACHYCEPHALOSAURUS

Pachycephalosaurus was the largest of a dinosaur group memorably called the bone heads or head-butters. More than eight metres long, and five metres standing upright, its remains are scarce and fragmentary. It roamed what is now western North America, 70 million years ago.

STIFF-BACKED
Strips of muscle anchored to the vertebrae ran from the base of the neck all the way down the back, to keep the spine straight and stiff.

Bony lumps on upper neck

Crown of skull bone was 25 centimetres thick

THE BONE-DOME
Pachycephalosaurus' head was topped by a massive "crash-helmet" of bone. As a form of defence, these dinosaurs may have charged at enemies. Or perhaps they butted each other to take charge of the herd, or a female at mating time, as rams do today.

External ear

THICK NECK
The vertebrae in *Pachycephalosaurus'* neck are thick and strong, and fit firmly, with minimal twisting. The muscles are big and powerful, too. This adds support to the theory that the head could absorb tremendous jarring shocks. The dinosaur's name means "thick-headed reptile".

Snout nodules

Small, serrated teeth to tear and shred plant foods

Five clawed fingers on hand

Muscle connecting hip to fibula (calf bone)

Muscle connecting hip to tibia (shin bone)

BIRD-LIKE
Large eyes and a long, beak-shaped mouth were further bird-like features. *Struthiomimus* may have chased after small lizards and other creatures, and also caught flying insects, grabbing them in mid-air with its mouth or long fingers.

Toothless jaws

BUILT FOR SPEED
Struthiomimus is known as the "ostrich mimic", and the parallels of long, muscular legs and feet are clear. It is possible this dinosaur sprinted as fast as its flightless bird-cousin of today – about 72 km/h.

Muscle connecting tail to femur (thigh bone)

Tibia (shin bone)

Femur (thigh bone)

Ankle joint

Foot bones

Large gripping claws

WELL BALANCED
The slim, lightweight body was perfectly balanced over the rear legs. The tail acted as a counterweight to the head and neck, and was used possibly as a steering rudder when running.

Toe bones

NO EARLY BIRD
Ostrich dinosaurs such as *Struthiomimus* lived towards the end of the Age of Dinosaurs, about 80-70 million years ago. This member of the family was about four metres long and stood slightly taller than an adult human.

Long grasping fingers

TINY, BUT SPEEDY
Hen-sized *Compsognathus* ("pretty-jaw") was one of the smallest dinosaurs. Yet it had the same long legs and slim, well-balanced head and tail of the bigger two-legged, fast-moving dinosaurs. It sped along the ground 140 million years ago in Europe, snapping and snatching small prey such as insects.

SLASH AND GNASH

IT WAS A DINOSAUR-EAT-DINOSAUR WORLD – but which dinosaurs were the vicious predators, and which were their terrified prey? Sharp teeth and pointy claws denote both the hunting weapons and defensive tools of the predator. A fine dinosaur example was the pack-hunting, human-sized, "terrible claw" *Deinonychus*. Its sharp, dagger-like claw on each foot could slash, maim, and dismember a victim with one deadly swing.

DEINONYCHUS
Less than two metres tall, and just over three metres long, the dromaeosaurid *Deinonychus* lived about 100 million years ago in western North America.

WOLF OF THE DINOSAUR AGE?
Several skeletons of *Deinonychus* were found together, indicating that these dinosaurs may have hunted in packs to tackle larger prey, as wolves hunt elk or reindeer today. Some would bite and scratch the victim, while others would slash at its vulnerable belly and disembowel it with their terrible claws.

TOE HOLD-UP
As *Deinonychus* moved along, it probably held the huge-clawed second toe up from the ground, to keep it razor sharp and poised for action. The third and fourth toes are large and strong, well suited for walking and running.

Muscles and tendons ready to contract...

...and contracted

Restraining ligaments

Pull of femoralis-tarsus and flexor digitorum muscles

QUICK FLICK CLAW
The clawed second toe was normally held up and back by ligaments and muscles. The toe-bending muscles and tendons stretched taut like a bowstring. When the muscles contracted, they released the power of the stretched tendons. Together, tendons and muscles flicked the toe bones and claw through a deadly, slashing arc.

Third toe

Fourth toe

Toe-flexing muscles

KNIFE-FLICKERS
The flexor digitorum and femoralis-tarsus (gastrocnemius) muscles contracted to flip the second-toe claw forward and down like a flick-knife.

"Terrible claw" on second toe

Claw-kicking tendons and muscles

UNDER WRAPS
Strap-like ligaments wrapped around the toe muscles and tendons, holding them in place.

Femoralis-tarsus muscle

Second toe has completed slashing movement

Flexible skin on toe

Tiny, spur-like first toe

Pubis

Hip muscles

Tibia (shin) bone

Thigh muscles

Third finger

Second finger

First finger

Flexible wrist

Radius and ulna (forearm bones)

HAVE A BITE
Deinonychus' fearsome curving teeth had knife-like edges. Its strong jaw muscles enabled it to wrap its mouth round the flesh of the bleeding, disembowelled victim and saw off bite-sized chunks.

THUMBS UP
The herbivore *Iguanodon* (p.8) had a peculiar spiky claw on its thumb. This may have been a jabber-stabber defence weapon. The three main hoof-like fingers were strong, for four-legged walking.

Spiky thumb

Three strong fingers

Flexible fifth finger

AT ARMS' LENGTH
Compared to similar dinosaurs, the upper arm and forearm of *Deinonychus* were relatively long and muscular. They may have held prey at arms' length, to make room for the kick-and-slash attack with the lower limbs.

HOLD TIGHT!
The shoulder muscles were large and strong, to hold down struggling prey.

GRAPPLING HOOKS
Three sharp, talon-like claws tipped *Deinonychus'* fingers. Roughened patches on the arm and finger bones suggest powerful musculature for moving them. Perhaps this hunter jabbed its finger claws into a potential meal, like grappling hooks.

Elbow joint

Digital artery

Ulnar artery

Radius and ulna bones

Jaw joint

Rear of skull

Neck vertebrae and muscles

Nasal holes

Long, narrow snout

CURIOUS TEETH
Baryonyx's strange dental plan comprised many sharp, crocodile-like teeth at the front of its long, narrow snout, and smaller pencil-type teeth at the rear. These suggest a piscivore (fish-eater) or perhaps the probing snout of a scavenger.

Powerful chest muscles under skin

Mandible (lower jaw bone)

Trachea (windpipe)

Oesophagus (gullet)

GONE FISHIN'
Although "heavy claw" *Baryonyx* may have fished England's rivers about 120 million years ago, it is a relatively recent dinosaur discovery. The enormous claw, 31 centimetres around its outside edge, was unearthed in a clay pit in Surrey, England in 1983. The reconstruction of this eight-metre long theropod shows this claw on the hand. Perhaps it was a fishing hook or a gaff to jerk shiny-scaled snacks from the shallows.

Heavy claw

Carpal (wrist) bones

Ulna

Radius

ARMOURED AND DANGEROUS

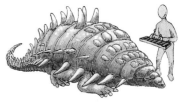

MEDIEVAL KNIGHTS-IN-ARMOUR were mere amateurs compared to the ankylosaurs, the "fused reptile" dinosaurs. The name refers to the way horny scales and plates of bone evolved and joined together to protect almost every part of their anatomy, except the ever-vulnerable belly. One subgroup, the ankylosaurids, included *Euoplocephalus* (p.16). The other ankylosaur subgroup were the nodosaurids, such as *Hylaeosaurus*, shown here. This tank-like reptile could have frightened away those who wanted to make a meal of it simply by squatting down on the ground and looking scary. Running away was probably out of the question. Ankylosaur armour was so thick that few predators could break through, but so heavy that it may have prevented a quick getaway.

HYLAEOSAURUS

Four metres long, and twenty times the weight of a human, this squat beast was one of the original *Dinosauria* named by Richard Owen in 1841. It lived 130 million years ago in southern England and northern France. The name means "woodland reptile" – some of its fossils were found in a forest.

Spine (see far right)

Blue dashed lines show a body part is pulled away

SETS OF SPIKES
Three double-rows of spikes, stuck in heavily-scaled skin, protected *Hylaeosaurus'* rear end. Dorsal spikes ran along the top of the tail, and lateral ones along each side.

Dorsal spikes

Lateral spikes

Joints between protective plates allowed flexibility

Intestines

Stomach

Lung

Heart

DEFENSIVE DINOSAUR
The nodosaurids such as *Hylaeosaurus* lacked a bony tail club, the weapon swung by *Euoplocephalus* (p.16). They may have defended themselves by running at enemies and jabbing them with their spikes. Perhaps they relied on their apperance alone to frighten off attackers.

KEEPING A LOW PROFILE
If it gripped the ground with its four-clawed legs, and bent its limbs, *Hylaeosaurus* would cling like a giant limpet – immoveable, and impregnable.

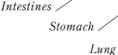

PROTECTION BASKET

The back of *Hylaeosaurus* had three types of protection. Long, curved plates of bone-reinforced skin curved from side to side like a row of saddles. Within these were embedded rounded lumps or nodules of bone, and sharper bony spikes. The whole structure was like an upturned, armoured basket.

HORNS AND FRILLS

One of the most famous dinosaurs is *Triceratops*, "three-horned face". It was a ceratopsid, member of a group that appeared late in the Age of Dinosaurs, only 100 million years ago. The solid neck frill was probably both a back-protector and an anchor for the jaw-closing muscles. Two long eyebrow horns and a shorter nose horn gave it its terrifying profile.

Twin eyebrow horns

Curved bony saddle

Rounded bony nodule

Single nose horn

Ribs (not attached to armour)

Parrot-like plant-snipping horny beak

Cervical vertebrae (not attached to armour)

Plant-slicing teeth

Mandible (lower jaw)

Jaw-closing capiti-mandibularis muscle

ONLY SKIN DEEP

The bony plates, lumps, and spikes of dinosaur armour were not part of the true skeleton, nor were they attached to it. Like a modern reptile's scales, they were embedded in the skin, as dermal bone. So by skinning a dinosaur, you would also remove its suit of armour.

Dense, compact bone

Softer, spongy bone

Skin and plate of dermal bone

Subcutaneous fibres and muscle

Fascial sheath (inner body lining)

Vertebral muscle blocks

Olfactory (smell) organ

Vertebral bones

Nasal passages

A BITE, AND A BREATH

Most ankylosaurs seem to have had a bony shelf or plate, the hard palate, between the nose and mouth. This would allow the creature to bite and chew food below the palate, while still being able to breathe through the nasal passages above it. No modern reptiles can do this – but you can.

Hard palate

Mouth

Trachea (windpipe)

Neck spike

Neck shield

Forehead plate

Eyebrow ridge protects eye

HOLES IN THE HEAD

WAS PREHISTORY NOISY? Reptiles today do not have vocal cords like mammals. The best they can do is a hiss or coarse roar, by blowing air up the windpipe and out through throat, nose, and mouth. However, fossils of one dinosaur group provide intriguing evidence that all was not quiet 70 million years ago. Some of the hadrosaurs possessed strange crests on their heads, and long, twisty nasal passages. These odd features may have been living wind instruments – the first big sound systems. The hadrosaurs roared and trumpeted their way through life, but who were they singing to? Probably each other!

Hole through to right nasal passage

Lower nasal passage

Middle nasal passage

Nostril

Beak-like front of mouth

Parasaurolophus may have made a reedy sound like a clarinet

Hole through to right nasal passage

Skull

Lower jaw

Airflow

Trachea (windpipe)

Neck vertebrae

Oesophagus (gullet)

PARASAUROLOPHUS

Parasaurolophus was about ten metres long, and, like *Edmontosaurus* and *Corythosaurus*, roamed mid-west North America 70-65 million years ago. The weird headgear of these hadrosaurs may have been brightly coloured, to act as a visual signal of status or maturity for other members of the herd. Fossils of female skulls have crests that are much smaller than those of the males.

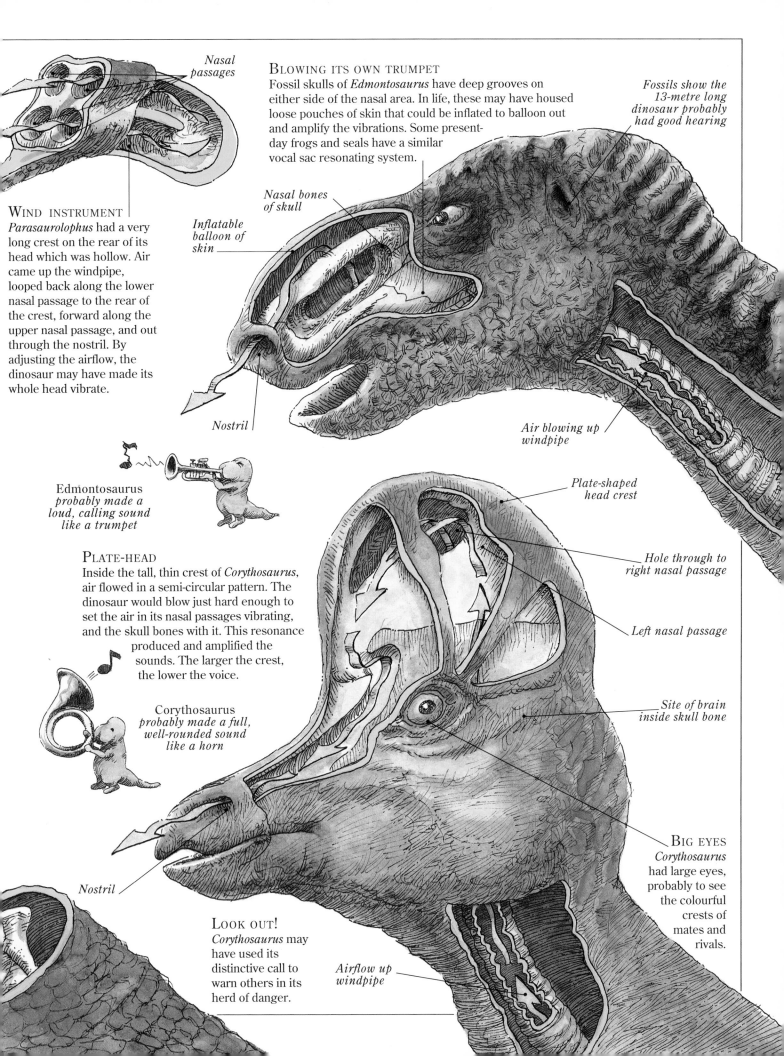

Nasal passages

BLOWING ITS OWN TRUMPET
Fossil skulls of *Edmontosaurus* have deep grooves on either side of the nasal area. In life, these may have housed loose pouches of skin that could be inflated to balloon out and amplify the vibrations. Some present-day frogs and seals have a similar vocal sac resonating system.

Fossils show the 13-metre long dinosaur probably had good hearing

Nasal bones of skull

Inflatable balloon of skin

WIND INSTRUMENT
Parasaurolophus had a very long crest on the rear of its head which was hollow. Air came up the windpipe, looped back along the lower nasal passage to the rear of the crest, forward along the upper nasal passage, and out through the nostril. By adjusting the airflow, the dinosaur may have made its whole head vibrate.

Nostril

Air blowing up windpipe

Edmontosaurus *probably made a loud, calling sound like a trumpet*

Plate-shaped head crest

PLATE-HEAD
Inside the tall, thin crest of *Corythosaurus*, air flowed in a semi-circular pattern. The dinosaur would blow just hard enough to set the air in its nasal passages vibrating, and the skull bones with it. This resonance produced and amplified the sounds. The larger the crest, the lower the voice.

Hole through to right nasal passage

Left nasal passage

Corythosaurus *probably made a full, well-rounded sound like a horn*

Site of brain inside skull bone

BIG EYES
Corythosaurus had large eyes, probably to see the colourful crests of mates and rivals.

Nostril

LOOK OUT!
Corythosaurus may have used its distinctive call to warn others in its herd of danger.

Airflow up windpipe

BRAINS AND BODIES

THE FOSSIL RECORD SUGGESTS that dinosaurs were probably not what we would call clever or intelligent. Overall, these ancient reptiles had big bodies and small brains, not unlike modern-day crocodiles. But this does not imply that all dinos were dumb, lumbering beasts. In fact, some may have been alert, fast-reacting, and programmed with a nerve-system library of instincts and reflexes which enabled them to survive for so long. *Stegosaurus* had a very small brain indeed. Yet it survived – and thrived – for millions of years.

BRIGHT SPARK...
Stenonychosaurus had a relatively large brain in a smallish body. This meant it probably had good control over body movements, fine coordination skills, sharp senses, and even capacity left over for a simple memory bank.

...DIM BULB?
Stegosaurus, on the other hand, was probably not capable of skilled and agile movements. Limited brain power coupled with sheer bulk would have led to slow reactions, with much of the body "running on automatic".

SMALL AND SPRIGHTLY
Stenonychosaurus was two metres long and had fast reflexes, which it would have used for hunting lizards and small mammals. The dinosaur's large eyes may indicate that it hunted mainly at dusk, or even in the dark.

Powerful hip and leg muscles

Brain

Spinal cord

Sharp-clawed grasping hands

STEGOSAURUS
Stegosaurus is the most famous small-brain dinosaur. This armoured mound of flesh and bone, weighing in at one-and-a-half tonnes, and more than seven metres long, was controlled by a lump of nerves the size of a hen's egg.

HOT PLATE, COLD PLATE
The double-row of leaf-like plates along the back may have been used for defence, or as part of this dinosaur's body temperature control system (see p.35).

Scapula (shoulder bone)

Neck vertebrae

Rib

Nerves branching from spinal cord

Spinal cord

Brain

BRAIN POWER
Stegosaurus' body weighed 20,000 times more than its brain. *Stenonychosaurus'* body was 500 times heavier than its brain. Your body is only 50 times heavier than your brain, which indicates that your nervous system is highly efficient compared with dinosaurs.

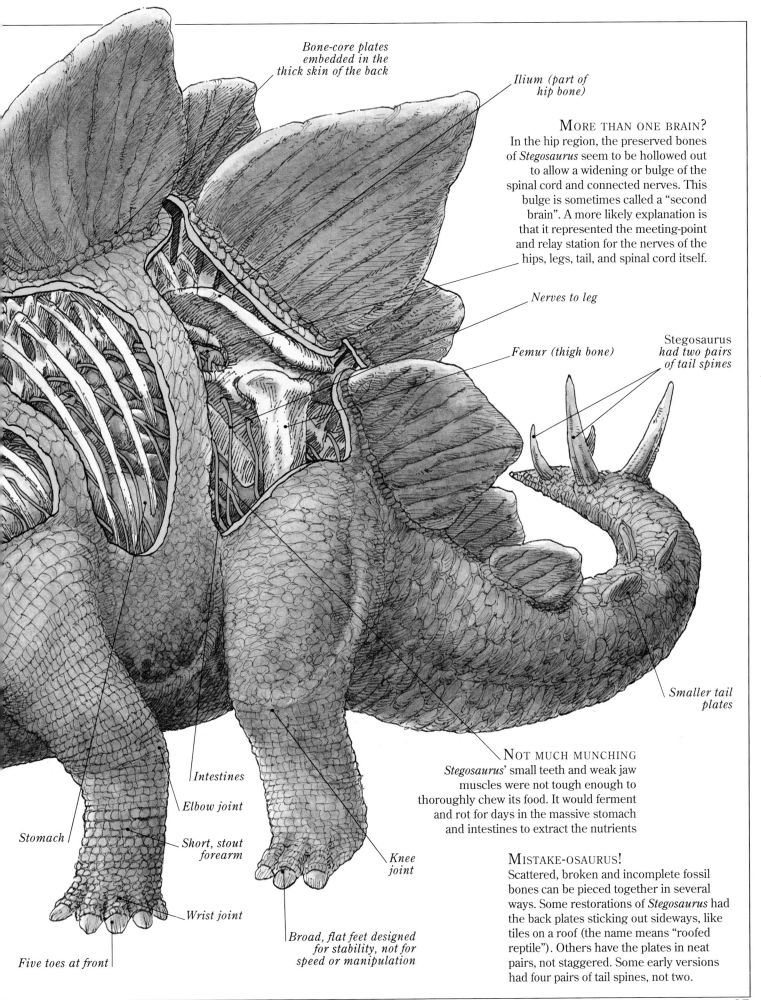

Bone-core plates
embedded in the
thick skin of the back

Ilium (part of
hip bone)

More than one brain?
In the hip region, the preserved bones of *Stegosaurus* seem to be hollowed out to allow a widening or bulge of the spinal cord and connected nerves. This bulge is sometimes called a "second brain". A more likely explanation is that it represented the meeting-point and relay station for the nerves of the hips, legs, tail, and spinal cord itself.

Nerves to leg

Femur (thigh bone)

Stegosaurus
had two pairs
of tail spines

Smaller tail
plates

Intestines

Elbow joint

Stomach

Short, stout
forearm

Knee
joint

Wrist joint

Five toes at front

Broad, flat feet designed
for stability, not for
speed or manipulation

Not much munching
Stegosaurus' small teeth and weak jaw muscles were not tough enough to thoroughly chew its food. It would ferment and rot for days in the massive stomach and intestines to extract the nutrients

Mistake-osaurus!
Scattered, broken and incomplete fossil bones can be pieced together in several ways. Some restorations of *Stegosaurus* had the back plates sticking out sideways, like tiles on a roof (the name means "roofed reptile"). Others have the plates in neat pairs, not staggered. Some early versions had four pairs of tail spines, not two.

SENSITIVE DINOSAURS

AFTER THE SQUIDGY DINOSAUR BRAIN rots away, a fossil called an endocast can form to fill the hollows in the skull. This is not quite a brain cast, since a living brain is surrounded by protective tissue and fluid. But there is sufficient similarity to show that dinosaurs had a general brain organization very like that of today's reptiles. Dinosaur endocasts also reveal chambers for the sense organs such as eyes, ears, and especially the nose, as seen in *Camarasaurus*. Far from being stupid, dinosaurs used sharp senses to help them survive.

CAMARASAURUS

A sauropod relation of *Brachiosaurus* and *Diplodocus*, *Camarasaurus* was an inhabitant of western North America about 140 million years ago. It was as tall as five people standing on each other's heads, as long as 12 people lying end to end, and as heavy as 500 people just sitting there.

BIG NOSE
Camarasaurus' skull consisted mainly of bony struts forming a large, airy chamber at the front, the nasal cavity. The nostrils were probably large and set high on the head. This gave ample space for copious amounts of aroma-bearing air to waft to and fro, on the way in and out of the lungs.

A WASHED-UP IDEA
Experts once thought sauropods lived underwater, using their long necks and high nostrils as snorkels. But fossils of sauropod footprints made in shallow water indicate otherwise.

DUCK-BILL DINO
Corythosaurus had the typical horny beak of the duck-billed hadrosaurs, and 900 chewing cheek teeth.

Nostril

— Brain

— Olfactory lobe

— Hairy olfactory nerves

— Optic nerve

— Nostril

— Nasal cavity

— Maxilla (upper jaw bone)

FORMIDABLE CHOPPERS
Camarasaurus had large, deep-rooted, chisel-like teeth all around its jaws. It probably reached up to the treetops with its long, flexible neck to chop off the leaves and twigs there.

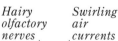

Olfactory lobe to brain

Hairy olfactory nerves

Swirling air currents

Food, potential mate, or enemy

Nostril

Trachea (windpipe to lungs)

Nasal cavity

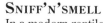

SNIFF'N'SMELL
In a modern reptile, the olfactory organ bears tufts of small hairs that project into the nasal cavity. Odorous substances inhaled with each sniff settle on the hairs and stimulate nerve signals. These are relayed to the olfactory lobes of the brain, where smells are identified.

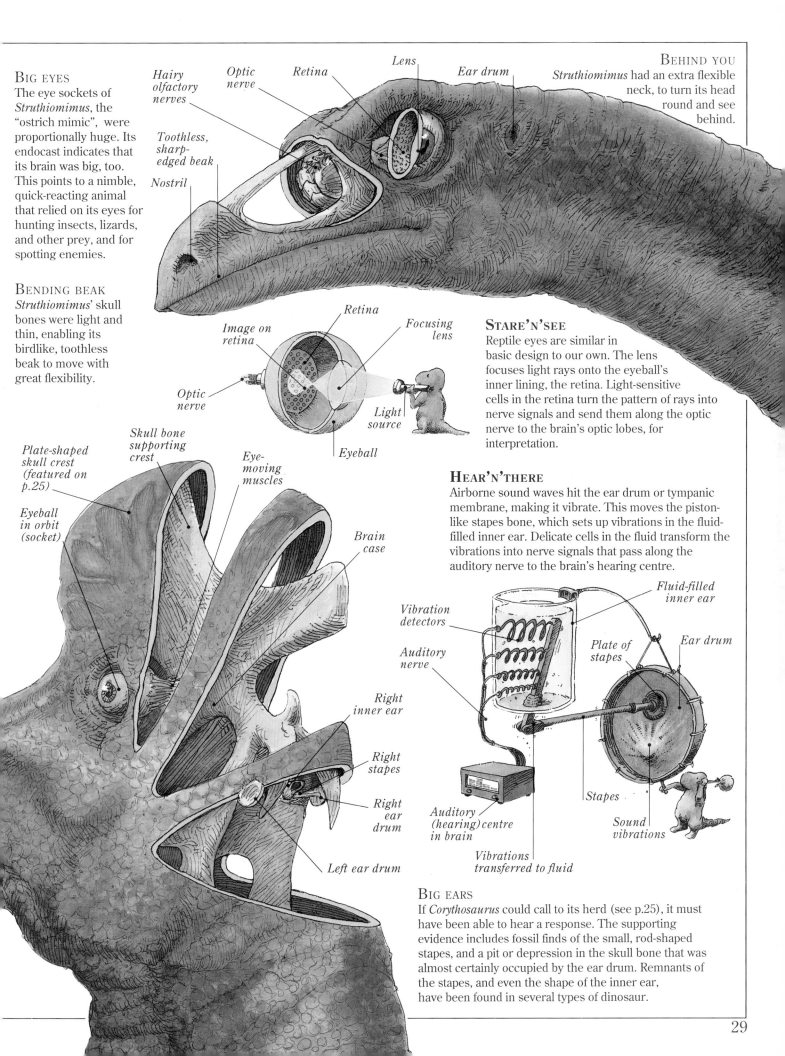

BIG EYES

The eye sockets of *Struthiomimus*, the "ostrich mimic", were proportionally huge. Its endocast indicates that its brain was big, too. This points to a nimble, quick-reacting animal that relied on its eyes for hunting insects, lizards, and other prey, and for spotting enemies.

BENDING BEAK

Struthiomimus' skull bones were light and thin, enabling its birdlike, toothless beak to move with great flexibility.

Hairy olfactory nerves

Optic nerve

Retina

Lens

Ear drum

Toothless, sharp-edged beak

Nostril

BEHIND YOU
Struthiomimus had an extra flexible neck, to turn its head round and see behind.

Retina

Image on retina

Focusing lens

Optic nerve

Light source

Eyeball

STARE'N'SEE

Reptile eyes are similar in basic design to our own. The lens focuses light rays onto the eyeball's inner lining, the retina. Light-sensitive cells in the retina turn the pattern of rays into nerve signals and send them along the optic nerve to the brain's optic lobes, for interpretation.

HEAR'N'THERE

Airborne sound waves hit the ear drum or tympanic membrane, making it vibrate. This moves the piston-like stapes bone, which sets up vibrations in the fluid-filled inner ear. Delicate cells in the fluid transform the vibrations into nerve signals that pass along the auditory nerve to the brain's hearing centre.

Plate-shaped skull crest (featured on p.25)

Skull bone supporting crest

Eye-moving muscles

Brain case

Eyeball in orbit (socket)

Right inner ear

Right stapes

Right ear drum

Left ear drum

Vibration detectors

Auditory nerve

Fluid-filled inner ear

Plate of stapes

Ear drum

Auditory (hearing) centre in brain

Vibrations transferred to fluid

Stapes

Sound vibrations

BIG EARS

If *Corythosaurus* could call to its herd (see p.25), it must have been able to hear a response. The supporting evidence includes fossil finds of the small, rod-shaped stapes, and a pit or depression in the skull bone that was almost certainly occupied by the ear drum. Remnants of the stapes, and even the shape of the inner ear, have been found in several types of dinosaur.

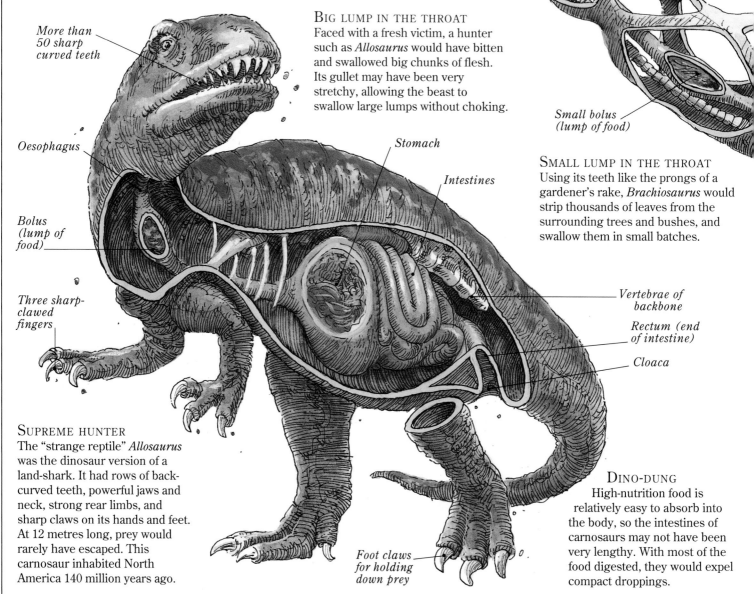

Food enters the oesophagus with every swallow

Trachea (windpipe)

Oesophagus (gullet)

DINOSAUR DIGESTION

LOOK AT THE AFRICAN GRASSLANDS TODAY. Lions and other carnivores laze in the shade, while wildebeest and other herbivores munch steadily and warily. The hunter's food may take some chasing, but it is the source of easily digested nutrients. Plant-eaters are stuck with chewing through mounds of herbage. The Age of Dinosaurs may have been remarkably similar. Giant plant-eaters kept an eye out for danger while they dined, while roaming packs of meat-eaters selected the young, old, and weak as their prey.

BRACHIOSAURUS
At 80 tonnes and with a length of 23 metres, this dinosaur was called "arm reptile" because of the enormous size of its forelimbs.

More than 50 sharp curved teeth

BIG LUMP IN THE THROAT
Faced with a fresh victim, a hunter such as *Allosaurus* would have bitten and swallowed big chunks of flesh. Its gullet may have been very stretchy, allowing the beast to swallow large lumps without choking.

Stomach

Intestines

Small bolus (lump of food)

Oesophagus

SMALL LUMP IN THE THROAT
Using its teeth like the prongs of a gardener's rake, *Brachiosaurus* would strip thousands of leaves from the surrounding trees and bushes, and swallow them in small batches.

Bolus (lump of food)

Vertebrae of backbone

Rectum (end of intestine)

Cloaca

Three sharp-clawed fingers

SUPREME HUNTER
The "strange reptile" *Allosaurus* was the dinosaur version of a land-shark. It had rows of back-curved teeth, powerful jaws and neck, strong rear limbs, and sharp claws on its hands and feet. At 12 metres long, prey would rarely have escaped. This carnosaur inhabited North America 140 million years ago.

Foot claws for holding down prey

DINO-DUNG
High-nutrition food is relatively easy to absorb into the body, so the intestines of carnosaurs may not have been very lengthy. With most of the food digested, they would expel compact droppings.

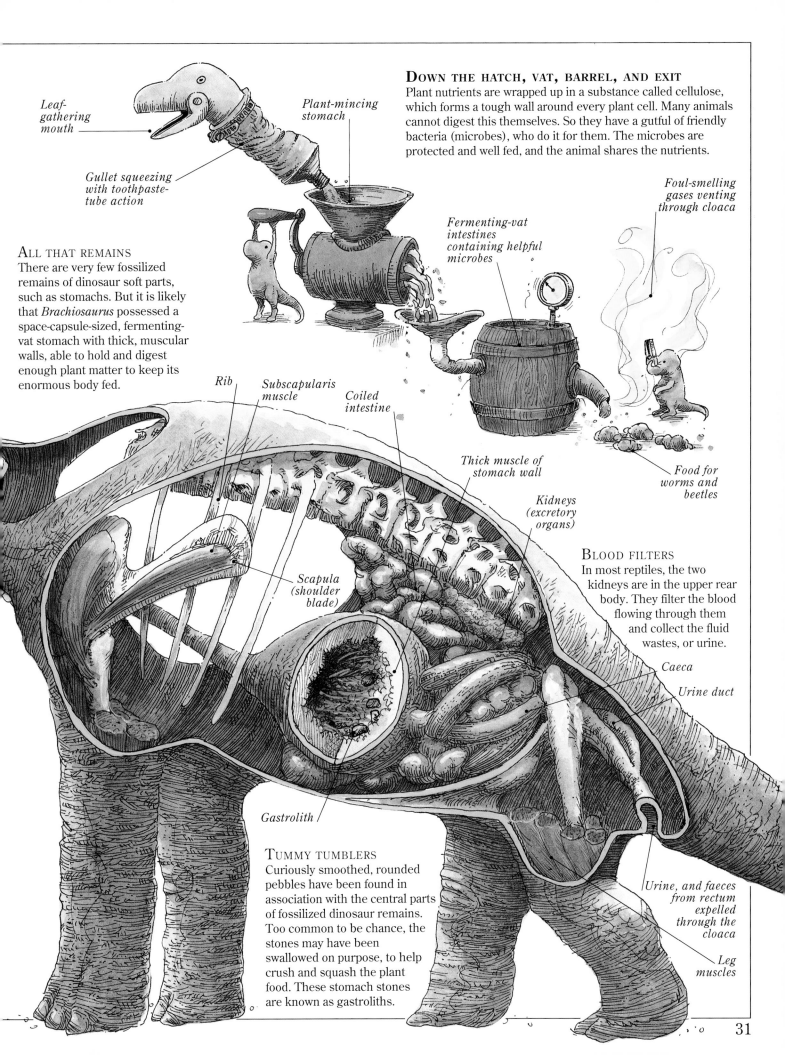

Leaf-gathering mouth

Plant-mincing stomach

Gullet squeezing with toothpaste-tube action

DOWN THE HATCH, VAT, BARREL, AND EXIT
Plant nutrients are wrapped up in a substance called cellulose, which forms a tough wall around every plant cell. Many animals cannot digest this themselves. So they have a gutful of friendly bacteria (microbes), who do it for them. The microbes are protected and well fed, and the animal shares the nutrients.

Fermenting-vat intestines containing helpful microbes

Foul-smelling gases venting through cloaca

ALL THAT REMAINS
There are very few fossilized remains of dinosaur soft parts, such as stomachs. But it is likely that *Brachiosaurus* possessed a space-capsule-sized, fermenting-vat stomach with thick, muscular walls, able to hold and digest enough plant matter to keep its enormous body fed.

Rib

Subscapularis muscle

Coiled intestine

Thick muscle of stomach wall

Food for worms and beetles

Kidneys (excretory organs)

Scapula (shoulder blade)

BLOOD FILTERS
In most reptiles, the two kidneys are in the upper rear body. They filter the blood flowing through them and collect the fluid wastes, or urine.

Caeca

Urine duct

Gastrolith

TUMMY TUMBLERS
Curiously smoothed, rounded pebbles have been found in association with the central parts of fossilized dinosaur remains. Too common to be chance, the stones may have been swallowed on purpose, to help crush and squash the plant food. These stomach stones are known as gastroliths.

Urine, and faeces from rectum expelled through the cloaca

Leg muscles

31

BREATHING AND BLOOD

A DINOSAUR'S OXYGEN SUPPLY probably came from breathed-in air. Two lungs absorbed the oxygen, which was then distributed around the body by the heart, blood vessels, and blood. Pushing blood around a body bigger than a truck was hard work for the heart of *Apatosaurus*. Its heart could not have worked like the partly divided heart of some of its reptile relatives. Otherwise the same immense pressure needed to push blood up to its brain would have forced blood into its delicate lungs and blown them apart. The heart must have been fully divided into two quite separate pumps, one powering a high-pressure circuit to the body, the other a low-pressure circuit to the lungs.

APATOSAURUS

This massive beast was 21 metres nose-to-tail, five metres high at its hips, and weighed 30 tonnes. Some of its fossils were once named *Brontosaurus*, but all specimens are now called *Apatosaurus*, or "deceptive reptile" – a good name for a dinosaur that confused the experts.

CAUDAL ARTERY

This huge blood vessel, probably wider than your entire leg, conveyed blood down to the muscles and bones in the dinosaur's tail.

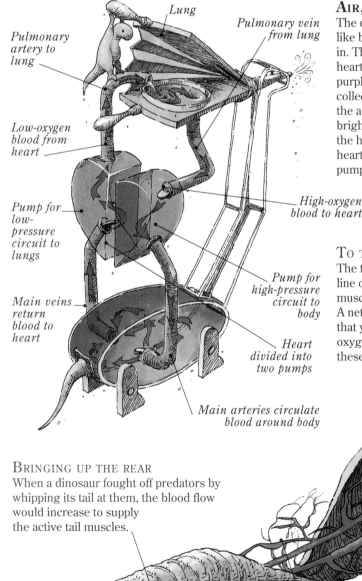

Lung

Pulmonary vein from lung

Pulmonary artery to lung

Low-oxygen blood from heart

Pump for low-pressure circuit to lungs

Main veins return blood to heart

High-oxygen blood to heart

Pump for high-pressure circuit to body

Heart divided into two pumps

Main arteries circulate blood around body

AIR, TO BLOOD, TO BODY

The dinosaur's lungs expand like bellows and suck fresh air in. The low-pressure side of the heart pumps stale, bluish-purple blood into the lungs to collect dissolved oxygen from the air. Refreshed and now bright red, the blood returns to the high-pressure side of the heart. From here, the blood is pumped around the dinosaur.

TO THE TIP OF THE TAIL

The tail of *Apatosaurus* had a long line of spinal bones, surrounded by muscles and covered in skin. A network of blood vessels (all that you can see here) carried oxygen and nourishment to all these structures.

Caudal vein

BRINGING UP THE REAR

When a dinosaur fought off predators by whipping its tail at them, the blood flow would increase to supply the active tail muscles.

Network of blood vessels in tail

Scaly skin covering tail

ELEPHANTINE FEET

Apatosaurus had short, splayed claws and stood flat-footed, in the manner of today's elephant. This spread its body weight – seven tonnes on each foot – over a wider area, to prevent the massive creature from sinking into soft ground.

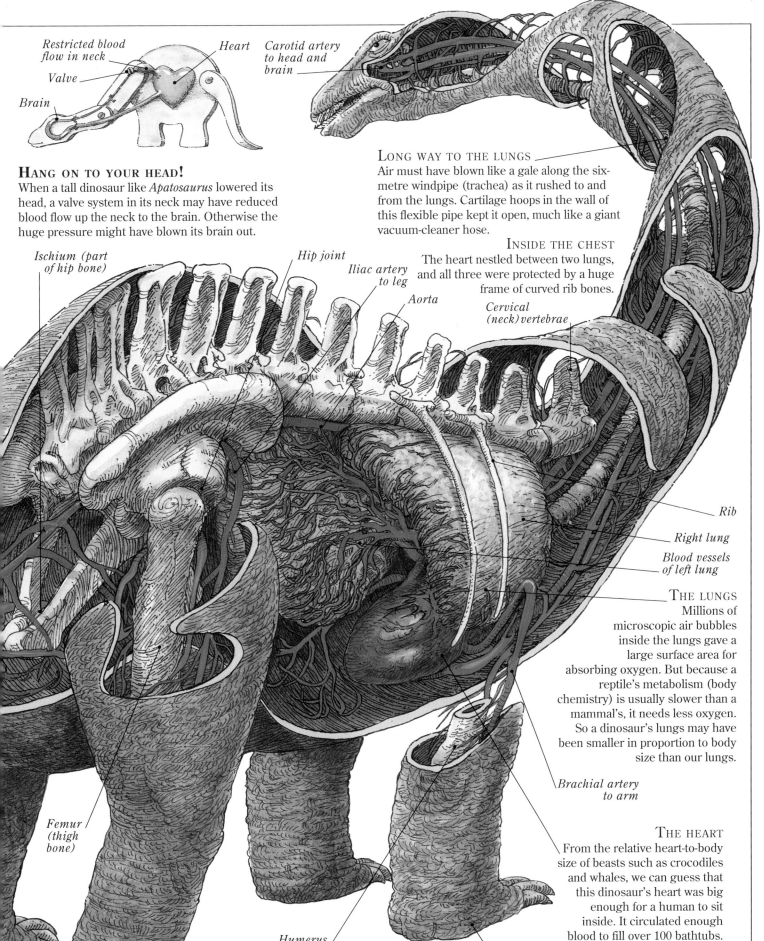

HANG ON TO YOUR HEAD!

When a tall dinosaur like *Apatosaurus* lowered its head, a valve system in its neck may have reduced blood flow up the neck to the brain. Otherwise the huge pressure might have blown its brain out.

Restricted blood flow in neck

Valve

Brain

Heart

Carotid artery to head and brain

LONG WAY TO THE LUNGS

Air must have blown like a gale along the six-metre windpipe (trachea) as it rushed to and from the lungs. Cartilage hoops in the wall of this flexible pipe kept it open, much like a giant vacuum-cleaner hose.

INSIDE THE CHEST

The heart nestled between two lungs, and all three were protected by a huge frame of curved rib bones.

Ischium (part of hip bone)

Hip joint

Iliac artery to leg

Aorta

Cervical (neck) vertebrae

Rib

Right lung

Blood vessels of left lung

THE LUNGS

Millions of microscopic air bubbles inside the lungs gave a large surface area for absorbing oxygen. But because a reptile's metabolism (body chemistry) is usually slower than a mammal's, it needs less oxygen. So a dinosaur's lungs may have been smaller in proportion to body size than our lungs.

Brachial artery to arm

THE HEART

From the relative heart-to-body size of beasts such as crocodiles and whales, we can guess that this dinosaur's heart was big enough for a human to sit inside. It circulated enough blood to fill over 100 bathtubs.

Femur (thigh bone)

Humerus (upper arm bone)

Five-clawed front foot

33

A HEATED DEBATE

MODERN REPTILES ARE COLD-BLOODED. Dinosaurs were reptiles. But were dinosaurs cold-blooded? Probably, but some experts are warming to other ideas. It is likely that most dinosaurs were cold-blooded, or to be more accurate, *ectothermic* ("warmth from without"). An ectotherm's body temperature depends on its surroundings. In hot weather it warms up, ready for action. In cold conditions it becomes slow and sluggish. However, many of today's reptiles can regulate their body temperature within certain limits by behavioural methods – basking in the sun, or cooling off in the shade. Maybe dinosaurs did the same – or, like *Spinosaurus*, kept a secret in their sails.

RAISING THE SAIL
Spinosaurus' huge back sail was supported by flattened bony planks. These are the enlarged dorsal processes, also called neural spines, projecting from the vertebrae (backbones). Some of these planks are almost two metres long – as tall as an adult human!

Dorsal processes grow progressively longer to form sail

Thin skin covering sail allows quick heat exchange

Ilium (part of hip bone)

Ilio-caudal muscle

SPINOSAURUS
This powerfully built, 12-metre carnivore dwelled in Africa, some 110 million years ago. Its fossils are not plentiful, but they indicate that it was a carnosaur cousin of the supreme North American hunter, *Allosaurus* (see p. 30).

Dorsal process of caudal vertebra (tail bone)

Transverse process of caudal vertebra

CENTRAL HEATING
As described above, reptiles and many other creatures – from insects to sharks – are ectothermic. Birds and mammals are *endothermic* ("warmth from within"). Their specialized metabolism (body chemistry) generates body heat that lets them stay active even in cold conditions.

Blood circulates just under the surface of the sail

Body heat lost through sail

RISE AND SHINE
The temperature control mechanism of *Spinosaurus* may have given it an edge over competitors, allowing it to get up and go in the early morning sun, before other cold-blooded creatures – including its prey – shook off the cool of the night.

Warmed blood travels to cold body

WARMING UP
The extravagant sail of *Spinosaurus* may have helped to regulate body temperature by acting as a heat exchanger. To warm itself rapidly, the beast stood sideways to the sun, and its sail soaked up the rays like a solar panel.

COOLING DOWN
If its body became too warm, *Spinosaurus* could stand in the breezy shade. The sail then worked as a radiator. Blood drew heat from the body, flowed through the sail, and dispersed the warmth to the passing air.

STEP ON IT
Spinosaurus had strong, pillar-like back legs. The huge claws on its feet may have been used to hold down its struggling prey while the dinosaur's mouth tore off chunks of flesh.

BLOOD BRANCHES
Vertebral blood vessels probably branched between the skin and supporting bone of the sail, to give a large surface area for heat exchange.

Vertebral branch of aorta (main artery)

ROUGHNECK
In common with its carnosaur relatives, *Allosaurus* and *Ceratosaurus*, *Spinosaurus* had a relatively large head. Its short, well-muscled neck must have been extremely powerful, so that it could support the head and twist it to wrench chunks out of animals clamped between its jaws.

Arch of aorta

Right carotid artery

Left carotid artery to head and brain

Sharp-clawed fingers

Short but powerful arms

Heart

Branching blood vessels

Bony core of plate

Plate base embedded in skin

Dorsal process of vertebra

THE ANSWER ON A PLATE?
As in *Spinosaurus*, temperature control is one explanation for the puzzling back plates of *Stegosaurus* shown here (see also p.26). Holes and grooves in their bony cores indicate the plates were covered with plentiful vessels, so that blood could ferry heat to or fro.

Three large foot claws

MORE PLATE DEBATE
Spinosaurus' sail and *Stegosaurus*' plates may have had little to do with body temperature. They could have been brightly patterned and coloured to frighten away enemies, or to advertise the dinosaur's strength and fitness to potential mates and breeding rivals.

Thin skin covering plate

Hip bone

Scaly skin

Vertebra

Vertebral artery

EGGS AND BABIES

DID DINOSAURS LAY EGGS, as their living reptile relatives do? Firm fossil evidence was unearthed in the 1920s in Mongolia's Gobi Desert. Here, numerous stony skeletons of the small frill-necked dinosaur *Protoceratops*, ranging from newborn babies to full-grown adults, were found in the sandstone layers – along with nests of perfectly fossilized eggs. These batches of rough-textured, oval eggs were laid carefully in scooped-out hollows in the sand, 80 million years ago. Since then, eggs of several dinosaur species have been discovered.

FIRST FRILLS
Protoceratops, "first horned face", was a forerunner of the ceratopsid or horned dinosaur group, which includes *Triceratops* with its huge neck frill. *Protoceratops*' frill was already quite large, but the facial horns that give the group its name were only just beginning to evolve, perhaps as a bump on the nose and ridges over the eyes.

Large neck frill

External ear

Eyebrow ridge

Nostril

SNACK SNIPPERS
Protoceratops was a herbivore. The front of the mouth was tipped with sharp, beak-shaped horn, for snipping up leaves and stems. Powerful jaw muscles worked scissor-like tooth batteries that cut tough plants into pieces. These were swallowed whole, since the teeth were no use for chewing.

Horny beak

Cheek teeth

Tongue

Yolk sac is main food store

Chorion just under shell surrounds rest of egg

Chalky eggshell reduces water loss

Body wastes stored in allantois

Food supply

Carbon dioxide waste seeps out of egg through shell, membranes, and fluids

Oxygen seeps into egg through shell, membranes, and fluids

Outer capsule

Container for body wastes

Protective cushioning

Albumen is extra food supply

Developing baby reptile

Amnion

Amniotic fluid cushions and cleans embryo

INSIDE THE EGG(S)
Amphibians lay their soft, jelly covered eggs in water – they could not survive elsewhere. A reptile egg, with its protective shell, was a great step forward to life on land. The developing baby fed on its yummy yolk in a private pool surrounded by three membranes – from inside out, the amnion, allantois, and chorion. Can you spot the parallels between the real egg and the fully fitted reptile nursery?

FOUR-FOOTED GAIT
Protoceratops almost certainly moved on all fours, supporting its massive weight on its short front and longer rear limbs.

Five-toed front foot

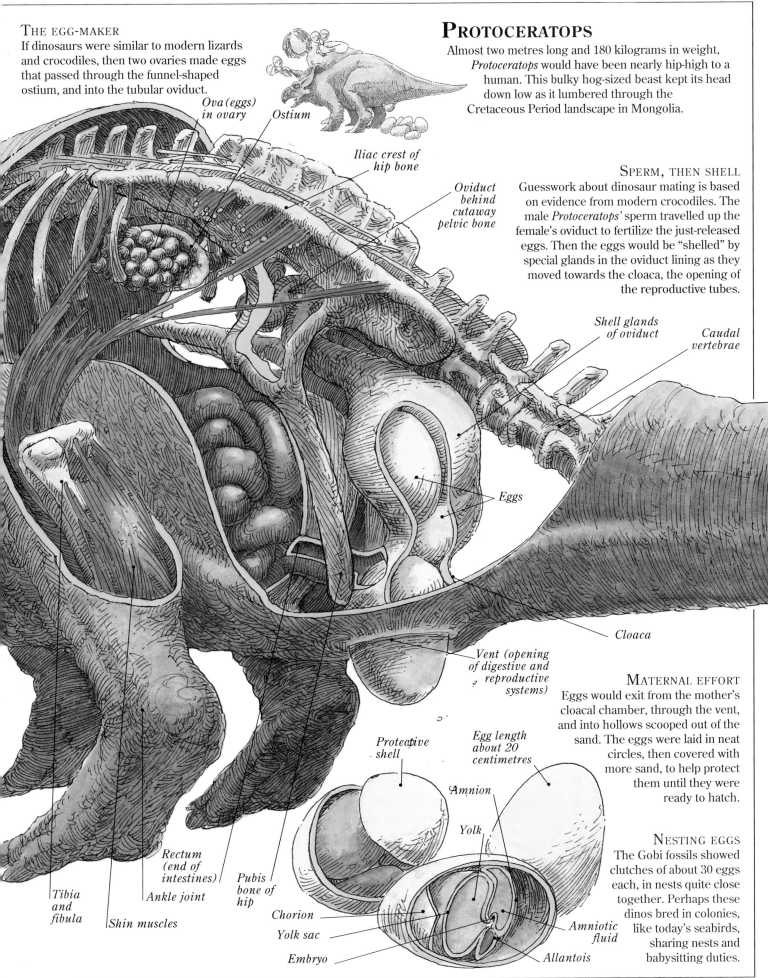

THE EGG-MAKER
If dinosaurs were similar to modern lizards and crocodiles, then two ovaries made eggs that passed through the funnel-shaped ostium, and into the tubular oviduct.

Ova (eggs) in ovary

Ostium

Iliac crest of hip bone

Oviduct behind cutaway pelvic bone

PROTOCERATOPS
Almost two metres long and 180 kilograms in weight, *Protoceratops* would have been nearly hip-high to a human. This bulky hog-sized beast kept its head down low as it lumbered through the Cretaceous Period landscape in Mongolia.

SPERM, THEN SHELL
Guesswork about dinosaur mating is based on evidence from modern crocodiles. The male *Protoceratops'* sperm travelled up the female's oviduct to fertilize the just-released eggs. Then the eggs would be "shelled" by special glands in the oviduct lining as they moved towards the cloaca, the opening of the reproductive tubes.

Shell glands of oviduct

Caudal vertebrae

Eggs

Cloaca

Vent (opening of digestive and reproductive systems)

MATERNAL EFFORT
Eggs would exit from the mother's cloacal chamber, through the vent, and into hollows scooped out of the sand. The eggs were laid in neat circles, then covered with more sand, to help protect them until they were ready to hatch.

Protective shell

Egg length about 20 centimetres

Amnion

Yolk

NESTING EGGS
The Gobi fossils showed clutches of about 30 eggs each, in nests quite close together. Perhaps these dinos bred in colonies, like today's seabirds, sharing nests and babysitting duties.

Amniotic fluid

Tibia and fibula

Ankle joint

Shin muscles

Rectum (end of intestines)

Pubis bone of hip

Chorion

Yolk sac

Embryo

Allantois

PREHISTORIC OCEANS

COULD DINOSAURS SWIM? A few may have paddled, waded, or even thrashed through the water to escape enemies. But no fossils clearly show dinosaurs had adaptations to an aquatic life. While dinosaurs roamed the land, however, more than a dozen major groups of reptiles took to the seas, lakes, and rivers. They probably abandoned life on land in independent bursts of evolution, braving the waves to find new food sources and avoid predators. Among these scaly swimmers were the dolphin-like *Ichythyosaurus*, the ancient sea turtle *Archelon*, and the plump-bodied *Plesiosaurus*.

FLEXI-FISHING ROD
With more than 30 vertebral bones in their necks, plesiosaurs probably made quick darting head movements to grab fish, spearing them on rows of pointy, interlocking teeth.

HOW TO FLOAT A REPTILE
With its buoyant lungs near the top of its body and heavy guts beneath, the resting plesiosaur could float right way up (below left). In order to float, as Greek scientist Archimedes later showed, the weight of water displaced by the creature (below right) should equal its total body weight.

Light, air-bubbled lungs

Heavy guts, maybe with stone ballast

Weight of water displaced = weight of plesiosaur

Cervical (neck) nerves

Heart

AQUA LUNGS
Plesiosaurs, like modern seals and whales, probably had relatively small lungs compared to those of land animals. Large, air-filled lungs would try to bob up to the surface like corks, giving the beast problems when it had to dive.

Oesophagus (gullet)

Cervical (neck) vertebrae

Trachea (windpipe)

UNDERSEA PIPELINE
Even at depths of two or three metres, water pressure increases considerably. The plesiosaur's trachea must have been reinforced against this extra pressure, to keep it open as the reptile surfaced like a whale for a breath of fresh air.

Phalanges (finger bones) of front right flipper

Enlarged shoulder and keel bones

Sterno-ulnar muscles

Ulna and radius (forearm bones)

Tarsals (wrist bones)

ROWER...
How did plesiosaurs swim? One idea is that plesiosaurs "rowed" with their flippers, moving them back and forth through the water in the same way that you row a boat with oars. Some mammals and tortoises swim this way.

...OR FLIER?
Marks on the shoulder and hip bones show that powerful paddle-waving muscles were anchored here. Their layout suggests that plesiosaurs "flew" underwater, by flapping their flippers up and down. This is how modern turtles and penguins swim.

THE FISH-LIKE SWISH
Ichthyosaurs, the "fish reptiles", probably used their fin-like limbs for steering but not for swimming. Propulsive power came from muscles along the sides of the backbones that worked the fish-like tail, swishing it strongly from side to side.

Pointed, stream-lined snout

Dorsal fin for stability

WATER BABIES
Unlike other reptiles, which lay eggs on land, a mother ichthyosaur gave birth to live young in the water – tail first, like modern porpoises.

KINKY TAIL
The tail bones (caudal vertebrae) bent down into the lower of the two tail lobes. This may have helped to drive the ichthyosaur head-up in the water with each tail swing. In sharks, the backbone kinks into the upper tail lobe.

Pelvic fin

Intestines

Stomach

Pectoral fin

Caudal (tail) vertebrae

Stiffening fin-ray bones

FISH SUPPERS
Like plesiosaurs and the fish-fancying dinosaur *Baryonyx* (p.21), ichthyosaurs had rows of slim, sharp teeth to grasp their slippery, wriggling prey.

CONVERGENT EVOLUTION
Sharks, other fast fish, dolphins, and ichthyosaurs have remarkably similar overall shapes, even though they are quite different inside. They are streamlined to slip through the water as speedily as possible. This outer similarity is termed convergent evolution.

Ribs

Intestines

Femur

PLESIOSAURUS
The first professional fossil hunter, Mary Anning, found not only the earliest known remains of an ichthyosaur, but also uncovered a nearly complete skeleton of the first *Plesiosaurus* ("near reptile") close to her home on the southern coast of England. The plesiosaurs, up to 14 metres long, thrived in the Jurassic and Cretaceous Periods.

Leg flipper

TAILING OFF
The typical plesiosaur tail was of medium length, tapering, and stiff. It was not used for propulsion, but was simply a smoothly pointed end to the body, to help with streamlining in the high-resistance aquatic environment.

DOUBLE PROTECTION
The protective bony shell is called the carapace on the back, and the plastron on the underside.

Vertebrae and ribs fused to inside of shell

Tiny, useless tail

Gastralia (stomach ribs)

BELLY BALLAST?
Plesiosaurs may have swallowed seabed pebbles, to give them ballast low in the body as well as to help grind up their food.

Leg flipper

Lung

Arm and hand bones in front flipper

HANDY FLIPPERS
The flipper bones resemble those in your own hand, though their shapes are broader and flatter to give an oar-like paddle.

EARLY TURTLE
Archelon, almost four metres long, paddled through the Cretaceous Period seas about 80 million years ago. It had large, flipper-like front limbs, a tough shell, and a curved, horny beak that may have trapped shellfish.

39

Fourth-finger bones

WING FINGER
Four incredibly long fouth-finger bones supported the wing. Another small bone near the claw, the pteroid, adjusted the shape of the wing to control flight speed.

PREHISTORIC SKIES

COULD DINOSAURS FLY? Although a few dinosaurs were undoubtedly nimble, and some could have jumped and leaped, none could actually fly. Soaring through the skies, over their land-bound dinosaur cousins and seagoing reptile relations, were the pterosaurs or "wing reptiles." These featherless fliers, including *Pteranodon*, appeared at the beginning of the Dinosaur Age, evolved and diversified, gradually declined, and finally died out with their flightless cousins some 65 million years ago.

FLYING FINGERS
Pterosaurs had four fingers; the fifth disappeared during their early evolution. The fourth finger supported the wing. The first three were flexible and claw-tipped, and could have been used for gripping, hanging, and climbing.

Pteroid bone

Supracoracoideus muscle

Coracoid bone

1 Reptilian runner, with four legs and horizontal body posture

HANGING AROUND
Narrow, long, and with sharp-clawed toes, the foot was better suited for hanging and gripping than for walking.

2 Glider, with stretchable skin flaps from forelimbs to tail

3 Steerable glider, with finger bones supporting wing

Femur (thigh bone)

Pelvic (hip) bones

Four digits on foot

Lungs

Pectoralis muscles

WING PULLERS
A flange on the breastbone, the cristospina (keel), anchored the powerful wing-pulling muscles.

FLAPPERS
Sets of muscles flapped the pterosaur wing down and back for the power stroke, and up on the recovery stroke. This provided the thrust and lift to keep the beast airborne.

Deltoideus pulls wing up

RUNNER TO FLIER
This sequence shows how pterosaurs may have evolved from four-legged reptiles, more than 220 million years ago. In the intermediate stages, the parachutelike skin flaps would be useful for leaping and gliding away from enemies, as in today's flying squirrels.

Long finger bone for wing adjustment

Supracoracoideus pulls wing up and forward

Pectoralis pulls wing down

Pteroid bone

Flexible ball-and-socket shoulder joint

Keel

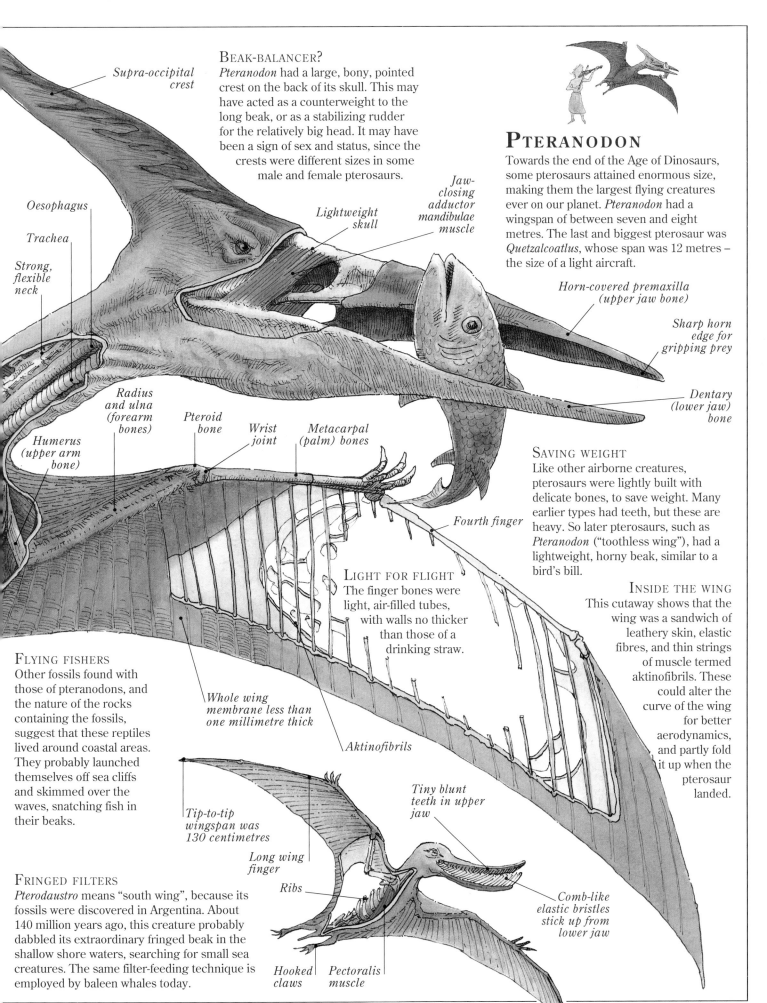

Supra-occipital crest

BEAK-BALANCER?
Pteranodon had a large, bony, pointed crest on the back of its skull. This may have acted as a counterweight to the long beak, or as a stabilizing rudder for the relatively big head. It may have been a sign of sex and status, since the crests were different sizes in some male and female pterosaurs.

Oesophagus

Trachea

Strong, flexible neck

Jaw-closing adductor mandibulae muscle

Lightweight skull

PTERANODON
Towards the end of the Age of Dinosaurs, some pterosaurs attained enormous size, making them the largest flying creatures ever on our planet. *Pteranodon* had a wingspan of between seven and eight metres. The last and biggest pterosaur was *Quetzalcoatlus*, whose span was 12 metres – the size of a light aircraft.

Horn-covered premaxilla (upper jaw bone)

Sharp horn edge for gripping prey

Dentary (lower jaw) bone

Humerus (upper arm bone)

Radius and ulna (forearm bones)

Pteroid bone

Wrist joint

Metacarpal (palm) bones

SAVING WEIGHT
Like other airborne creatures, pterosaurs were lightly built with delicate bones, to save weight. Many earlier types had teeth, but these are heavy. So later pterosaurs, such as *Pteranodon* ("toothless wing"), had a lightweight, horny beak, similar to a bird's bill.

Fourth finger

LIGHT FOR FLIGHT
The finger bones were light, air-filled tubes, with walls no thicker than those of a drinking straw.

INSIDE THE WING
This cutaway shows that the wing was a sandwich of leathery skin, elastic fibres, and thin strings of muscle termed aktinofibrils. These could alter the curve of the wing for better aerodynamics, and partly fold it up when the pterosaur landed.

FLYING FISHERS
Other fossils found with those of pteranodons, and the nature of the rocks containing the fossils, suggest that these reptiles lived around coastal areas. They probably launched themselves off sea cliffs and skimmed over the waves, snatching fish in their beaks.

Whole wing membrane less than one millimetre thick

Aktinofibrils

Tip-to-tip wingspan was 130 centimetres

Long wing finger

Tiny blunt teeth in upper jaw

Ribs

Comb-like elastic bristles stick up from lower jaw

FRINGED FILTERS
Pterodaustro means "south wing", because its fossils were discovered in Argentina. About 140 million years ago, this creature probably dabbled its extraordinary fringed beak in the shallow shore waters, searching for small sea creatures. The same filter-feeding technique is employed by baleen whales today.

Hooked claws

Pectoralis muscle

41

CREEPY-CRAWLIES

WHAT'S OLDER THAN A DINOSAUR? Long before any backboned creatures – whether amphibian or reptile – set foot on land, invertebrates (animals without backbones) crept across the Earth. Among the first were arthropods, animals with a hard outer body casing and jointed legs. They included centipedes, millipedes, mites, ticks, scorpions, and insects. With a 400-million-year history, land arthropods far outlived the dinosaurs, and still survive in incredible numbers. Today these small scurriers are sometimes called "minibeasts". But some minibeasts once reached maxi-sizes – this centipede was longer than your leg!

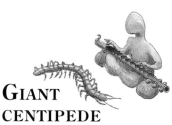

GIANT CENTIPEDE

Centipedes make up the group Chilopoda. They first crawled the land 250 million years ago. Today these creeping creatures grow to about 25 centimetres long, but their ancient cousins reached almost one metre in length.

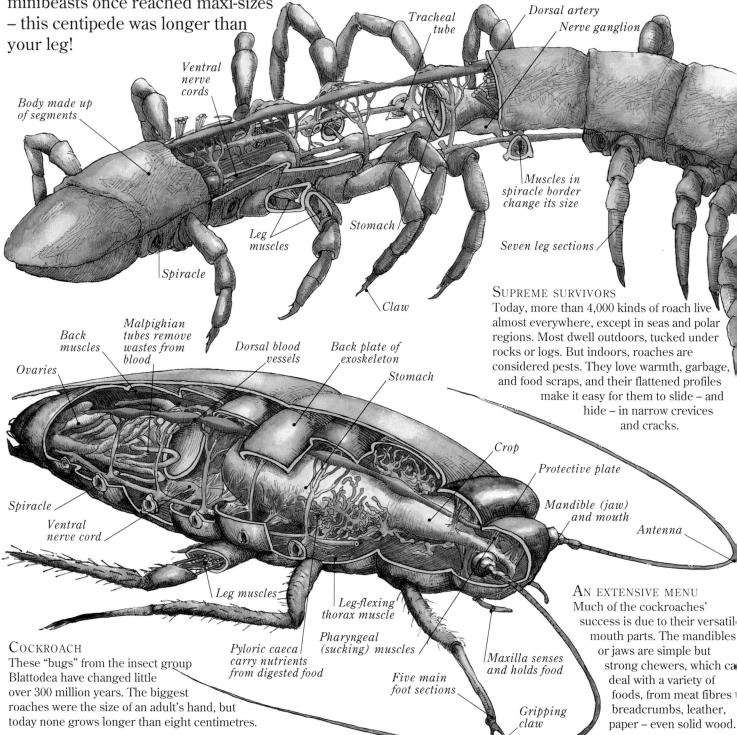

Tracheal tube

Dorsal artery

Nerve ganglion

Ventral nerve cords

Body made up of segments

Muscles in spiracle border change its size

Leg muscles

Stomach

Seven leg sections

Spiracle

Claw

Back muscles

Malpighian tubes remove wastes from blood

Ovaries

Dorsal blood vessels

Back plate of exoskeleton

Stomach

Spiracle

Ventral nerve cord

Crop

Protective plate

Mandible (jaw) and mouth

Antenna

Leg muscles

Leg-flexing thorax muscle

Pharyngeal (sucking) muscles

Maxilla senses and holds food

Pyloric caeca carry nutrients from digested food

Five main foot sections

Gripping claw

SUPREME SURVIVORS

Today, more than 4,000 kinds of roach live almost everywhere, except in seas and polar regions. Most dwell outdoors, tucked under rocks or logs. But indoors, roaches are considered pests. They love warmth, garbage, and food scraps, and their flattened profiles make it easy for them to slide – and hide – in narrow crevices and cracks.

AN EXTENSIVE MENU

Much of the cockroaches' success is due to their versatil[e] mouth parts. The mandibles or jaws are simple but strong chewers, which ca[n] deal with a variety of foods, from meat fibres breadcrumbs, leather, paper – even solid wood.

COCKROACH

These "bugs" from the insect group Blattodea have changed little over 300 million years. The biggest roaches were the size of an adult's hand, but today none grows longer than eight centimetres.

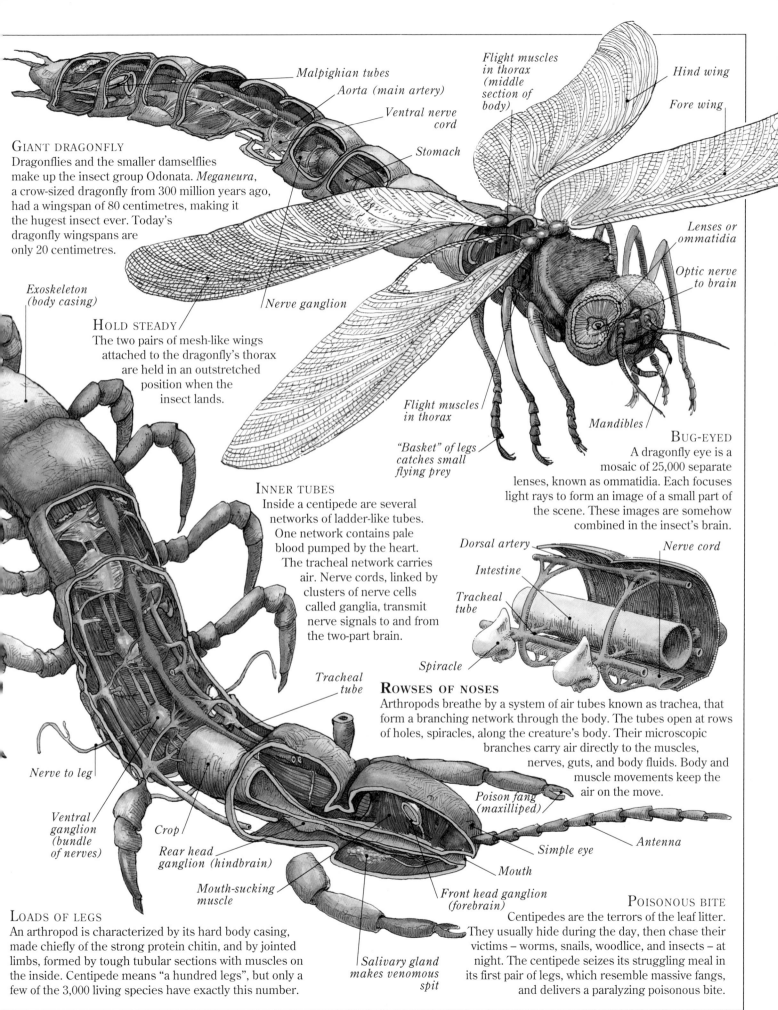

Malpighian tubes

Aorta (main artery)

Ventral nerve cord

Stomach

Flight muscles in thorax (middle section of body)

Hind wing

Fore wing

GIANT DRAGONFLY
Dragonflies and the smaller damselflies make up the insect group Odonata. *Meganeura*, a crow-sized dragonfly from 300 million years ago, had a wingspan of 80 centimetres, making it the hugest insect ever. Today's dragonfly wingspans are only 20 centimetres.

Exoskeleton (body casing)

Nerve ganglion

Lenses or ommatidia

Optic nerve to brain

HOLD STEADY
The two pairs of mesh-like wings attached to the dragonfly's thorax are held in an outstretched position when the insect lands.

Flight muscles in thorax

"Basket" of legs catches small flying prey

Mandibles

BUG-EYED
A dragonfly eye is a mosaic of 25,000 separate lenses, known as ommatidia. Each focuses light rays to form an image of a small part of the scene. These images are somehow combined in the insect's brain.

INNER TUBES
Inside a centipede are several networks of ladder-like tubes. One network contains pale blood pumped by the heart. The tracheal network carries air. Nerve cords, linked by clusters of nerve cells called ganglia, transmit nerve signals to and from the two-part brain.

Dorsal artery

Intestine

Tracheal tube

Nerve cord

Spiracle

Tracheal tube

ROWSES OF NOSES
Arthropods breathe by a system of air tubes known as trachea, that form a branching network through the body. The tubes open at rows of holes, spiracles, along the creature's body. Their microscopic branches carry air directly to the muscles, nerves, guts, and body fluids. Body and muscle movements keep the air on the move.

Nerve to leg

Ventral ganglion (bundle of nerves)

Crop

Rear head ganglion (hindbrain)

Mouth-sucking muscle

Poison fang (maxilliped)

Simple eye

Antenna

Mouth

Front head ganglion (forebrain)

Salivary gland makes venomous spit

LOADS OF LEGS
An arthropod is characterized by its hard body casing, made chiefly of the strong protein chitin, and by jointed limbs, formed by tough tubular sections with muscles on the inside. Centipede means "a hundred legs", but only a few of the 3,000 living species have exactly this number.

POISONOUS BITE
Centipedes are the terrors of the leaf litter. They usually hide during the day, then chase their victims – worms, snails, woodlice, and insects – at night. The centipede seizes its struggling meal in its first pair of legs, which resemble massive fangs, and delivers a paralyzing poisonous bite.

FUR AND FEATHER

FUR MEANS MAMMAL, and feathers mean bird. But it's not always so clear-cut. Extinct animals must be classified on the basis of their fossil remains. From the details of its teeth, jaw, and ear bones, we know that *Probelesodon* shown here is technically a reptile. Yet its fossils imply that it was so far along the road to becoming a mammal, it had fur and whiskers. The famous flying *Archaeopteryx* also had reptilian features, such as teeth, wing claws, and a chain of tail bones, which modern birds lack. But its fossilized feathers mark it out as the earliest known bird.

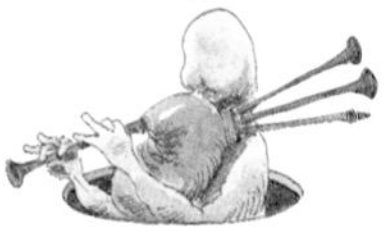

ARCHAEOPTERYX

Only six fossil specimens of the chicken-sized "ancient wing" have been found, all from southeast Germany. Feathers aside, they are so similar to reptiles that some were first identified as small pterosaurs, or dinosaurs such as *Compsognathus*. The remains are 150 million years old.

FORTUNATE PRESERVATION

The *Archaeopteryx* fossils are found in fine-grained limestone, which preserved the details of the feather shafts and barbs. The ancient feathers share aerodynamic flight features with those of modern birds, but they may have also served for protection, insulation, or as a display to enemies or mates.

Row of small teeth

Caudal (tail) vertebrae

Tail muscles

PROBABLE-ESODON!

Nobody knows what the inner parts of creatures such as *Probelesodon* actually looked like. But its internal organs probably followed the overall reptile body plan, with a heart, lungs, intestines, and kidneys. This is very similar to a mammal's body plan.

Bladder

Femur (thigh bone)

Hip joint

Pelvic bones

Kidney

WHY FUR?

A furry covering is flexible, yet protective. It can be patterned and coloured to camouflage its owner. But its main benefit may be that fur traps air and creates an insulating blanket. This keeps out intense cold and conserves body heat. So an endothermic (warm-blooded) animal can stay active when the cold-blooded ectotherms, like most reptiles, are too cool to move.

Intestines

Stomach

Knee joint

Femoro-tarsal muscles

Lungs

Heart

Humerus

Elbow joint

Claws on rear foot

PROBELESODON

This agile, terrier-sized reptile lived about 220 million years ago in South America. *Probelesodon* ("before lovely tooth) was a member of the cynodonts ("dog teeth"), an advanced subgroup of the mammal-like reptile group.

Five claws on front foot

ARM TO WING

Archaeopteryx's front limb was midway between ancient reptile and modern bird. A bird's wing is mostly upper-arm and forearm bones; wrist and hand are small. In *Archaeopteryx* the hand is still large, topped with three clawed digits or fingers.

Digit 1

Digit 2

Digit 3

Wrist

Radius and ulna
(forearm bones)

Humerus

Layers of
feathers

Caudal
vertebrae

Heart

Pelvis

Cloaca

Lung

Stomach

DID "ARCHY" FLY?

Archaeopteryx may have been an active, flapping flier. The feathers are aerodynamically designed, and there is a furcula (wishbone) in the chest, which may have anchored wing-moving muscles. But the sternum (breastbone) that holds the main flapping muscles in modern birds had not yet evolved. Instead *Archaeopteryx* had belly ribs, like some dinosaurs.

Tibia and
fibula

One claw
faces back

Three claws
face forwards

STRONG LEGS

Archaeopteryx was probably a speedy sprinter on the ground. Its long, strong legs were similar to those of a small running dinosaur.

Furcula
(wishbone)

Oesophagus (gullet)

Cervical vertebrae

Cranium
(brain case)

THEY'RE THE PITS

Probelesodon's preserved skull shows tiny pits in the snout bone. These are characteristic of the holes in mammal skulls where nerves and blood vessels pass to the roots of extra-large hairs – whiskers. If there were whiskers, there were probably body hairs.

Vibrissae
(whiskers)

Nostrils

Pits in
snout bone

Width of gap
registers in brain

Whisker bumps
into objects

Sensitive nerve
endings

JAW JOINT

A fossil jaw joint can tell you whether its owner was a reptile or a mammal. In reptiles, the articular bone of the lower jaw hinged to the quadrate bone of the skull. In mammals these two bones became part of the sound-conducting chain of bones in the inner ear.

Dog-like
canine
tooth

MIND THE GAP

A mammal's whiskers have movement-sensitive nerve endings wrapped around their roots. As a whisker tilts, the nerve endings signal to the brain, which forms a touch-picture of obstructions and gaps ahead. So the mammal can feel its way along even in darkness. Perhaps *Probelesodon* had the same system.

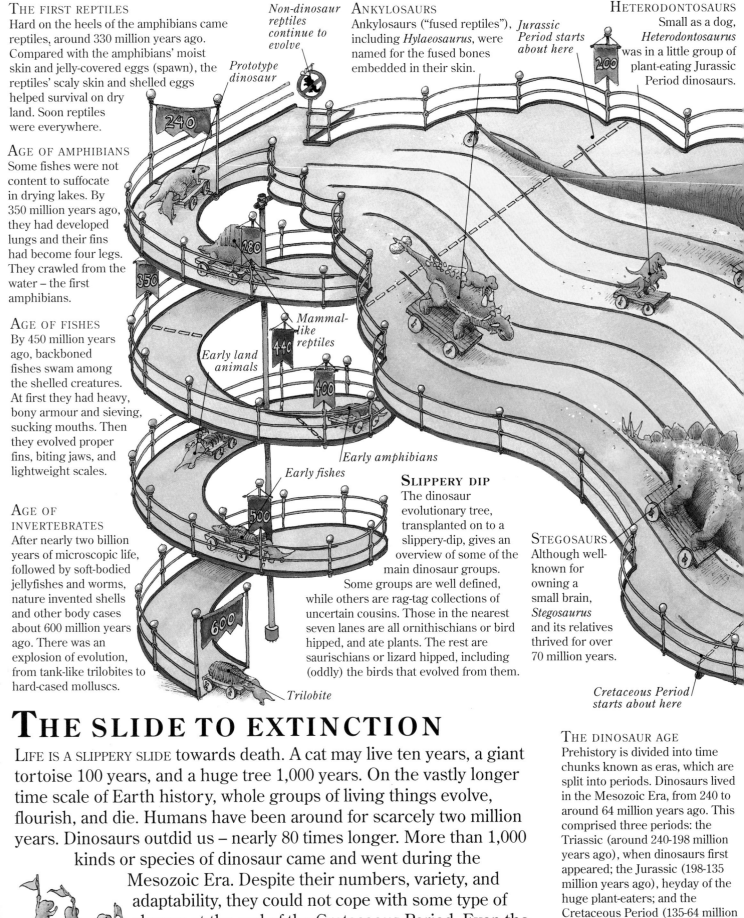

THE FIRST REPTILES
Hard on the heels of the amphibians came reptiles, around 330 million years ago. Compared with the amphibians' moist skin and jelly-covered eggs (spawn), the reptiles' scaly skin and shelled eggs helped survival on dry land. Soon reptiles were everywhere.

AGE OF AMPHIBIANS
Some fishes were not content to suffocate in drying lakes. By 350 million years ago, they had developed lungs and their fins had become four legs. They crawled from the water – the first amphibians.

AGE OF FISHES
By 450 million years ago, backboned fishes swam among the shelled creatures. At first they had heavy, bony armour and sieving, sucking mouths. Then they evolved proper fins, biting jaws, and lightweight scales.

AGE OF INVERTEBRATES
After nearly two billion years of microscopic life, followed by soft-bodied jellyfishes and worms, nature invented shells and other body cases about 600 million years ago. There was an explosion of evolution, from tank-like trilobites to hard-cased molluscs.

Non-dinosaur reptiles continue to evolve

Prototype dinosaur

ANKYLOSAURS
Ankylosaurs ("fused reptiles"), including *Hylaeosaurus*, were named for the fused bones embedded in their skin.

Jurassic Period starts about here

HETERODONTOSAURS
Small as a dog, *Heterodontosaurus* was in a little group of plant-eating Jurassic Period dinosaurs.

Mammal-like reptiles

Early land animals

Early amphibians

Early fishes

Trilobite

SLIPPERY DIP
The dinosaur evolutionary tree, transplanted on to a slippery-dip, gives an overview of some of the main dinosaur groups. Some groups are well defined, while others are rag-tag collections of uncertain cousins. Those in the nearest seven lanes are all ornithischians or bird hipped, and ate plants. The rest are saurischians or lizard hipped, including (oddly) the birds that evolved from them.

STEGOSAURS
Although well-known for owning a small brain, *Stegosaurus* and its relatives thrived for over 70 million years.

Cretaceous Period starts about here

THE SLIDE TO EXTINCTION

LIFE IS A SLIPPERY SLIDE towards death. A cat may live ten years, a giant tortoise 100 years, and a huge tree 1,000 years. On the vastly longer time scale of Earth history, whole groups of living things evolve, flourish, and die. Humans have been around for scarcely two million years. Dinosaurs outdid us – nearly 80 times longer. More than 1,000 kinds or species of dinosaur came and went during the Mesozoic Era. Despite their numbers, variety, and adaptability, they could not cope with some type of change at the end of the Cretaceous Period. Even the ultra-successful dinosaurs succumbed in the end.

THE DINOSAUR AGE
Prehistory is divided into time chunks known as eras, which are split into periods. Dinosaurs lived in the Mesozoic Era, from 240 to around 64 million years ago. This comprised three periods: the Triassic (around 240-198 million years ago), when dinosaurs first appeared; the Jurassic (198-135 million years ago), heyday of the huge plant-eaters; and the Cretaceous Period (135-64 million years ago), which closed with their extinction.

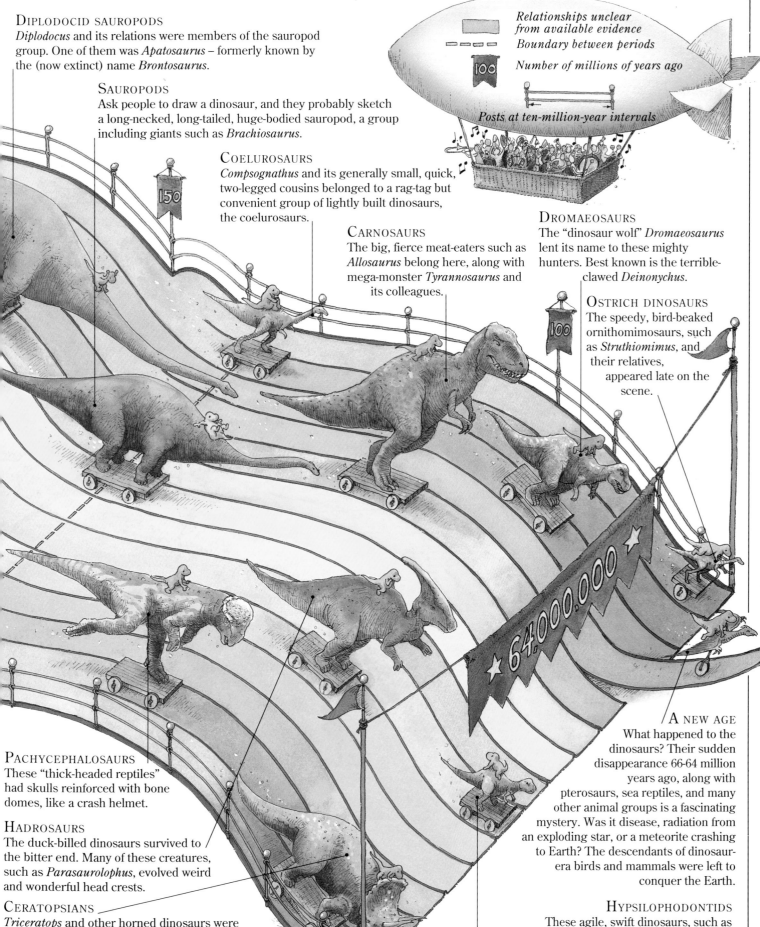

DIPLODOCID SAUROPODS
Diplodocus and its relations were members of the sauropod group. One of them was *Apatosaurus* – formerly known by the (now extinct) name *Brontosaurus*.

SAUROPODS
Ask people to draw a dinosaur, and they probably sketch a long-necked, long-tailed, huge-bodied sauropod, a group including giants such as *Brachiosaurus*.

COELUROSAURS
Compsognathus and its generally small, quick, two-legged cousins belonged to a rag-tag but convenient group of lightly built dinosaurs, the coelurosaurs.

CARNOSAURS
The big, fierce meat-eaters such as *Allosaurus* belong here, along with mega-monster *Tyrannosaurus* and its colleagues.

DROMAEOSAURS
The "dinosaur wolf" *Dromaeosaurus* lent its name to these mighty hunters. Best known is the terrible-clawed *Deinonychus*.

OSTRICH DINOSAURS
The speedy, bird-beaked ornithomimosaurs, such as *Struthiomimus*, and their relatives, appeared late on the scene.

Relationships unclear from available evidence

Boundary between periods

Number of millions of years ago

Posts at ten-million-year intervals

150

100

100

64.000.000

PACHYCEPHALOSAURS
These "thick-headed reptiles" had skulls reinforced with bone domes, like a crash helmet.

HADROSAURS
The duck-billed dinosaurs survived to the bitter end. Many of these creatures, such as *Parasaurolophus*, evolved weird and wonderful head crests.

CERATOPSIANS
Triceratops and other horned dinosaurs were just getting started with their evolution, when the Great Extinction cut them short.

A NEW AGE
What happened to the dinosaurs? Their sudden disappearance 66-64 million years ago, along with pterosaurs, sea reptiles, and many other animal groups is a fascinating mystery. Was it disease, radiation from an exploding star, or a meteorite crashing to Earth? The descendants of dinosaur-era birds and mammals were left to conquer the Earth.

HYPSILOPHODONTIDS
These agile, swift dinosaurs, such as *Hypsilophodon*, had specialized teeth to cope with Cretaceous Period vegetation.

47

INDEX

A

Allosaurus 12, 30, 34, 35, 47
Anatosaurus 10, 11, 14
Anchisaurus 14
ankylosaurs 17, 22, 46
Anning, Mary 39
Apatosaurus 12, 14, 32-33, 47
Archaeopteryx 44, 45
Archelon 38, 39
armour 22-23, ankylosaurs 46,
    Euoplocephalus 16, fishes 46,
    Hylaeosaurus 22, 23,
    Stegosaurus 26
arteries 32, *Apatosaurus* 33,
    centipede 42, *Meganeura* 43,
    Spinosaurus 35

B

babies 36, 39
Baryonyx 21, 39
bird 44, 45
blood 32-33, 34
blood vessels: *Apatosaurus* 32,
    cockroach 42, *Spinosaurus* 35
Brachiosaurus 14, 28, 30-31, 47
brains 26-27, *Apatosaurus* 32, 33,
    Camarasaurus 28,
    Edmontosaurus 25,
    Mamenchisaurus 13,
    Spinosaurus 35, *Stegosaurus* 26,
    Stenonychosaurus 26,
    Struthiomimus 29
breathing 32-33
Brontosaurus 32, 47

C

Camarasaurus 28
carnosaurs 30, 34, 35, 47
centipedes 42, 43
ceratopsian dinosaurs 23, 36, 47
Ceratosaurus 12, 35
Chilopoda 43
claws: *Allosaurus* 30,
    Apatosaurus 32, 33,
    Archaeopteryx 44, 45,
    Baryonyx 21, centipede 42,
    cockroach 42,
    Deinonychus 20, 21,
    Diplodocus 16, *Iguanodon* 8, 9,
    Probelesodon 44, *Pteranodon* 40,
    Spinosaurus 35,
    Stenonychosaurus 26,
    Tyrannosaurus 11
cloaca 30, 31, 37, 45
cockroach 42
coelurosaurs 47
Compsognathus 19, 44, 47
Corythosaurus 24, 25, 28, 29
crests 24, 25, 41, 47
cynodonts 44

D

Deinonychus 20-21, 47
Dimetrodon 46
diplodocid dinosaurs 47
Diplodocus 12-14, 15, 18, 28
dragonflies 43
dromaeosaurid dinosaurs 20, 47
droppings 6, 30

E

ears 28, 29, 36, 45
ectotherms and endotherms 34, 44
Edmontosaurus 24, 25
eggs 6, 36, 37, 46
Euoplocephalus 16, 17, 22
exoskeleton 42, 43
eyes 28, *Corythosaurus* 25,
    Hylaeosaurus 23, *Meganeura* 43,
    Stenonychosaurus 26,
    Struthiomimus 29

F

feathers 44, 45
femur: *Apatosaurus* 33,
    Euoplocephalus 17,
    Iguanodon 8,
    Pachycephalosaurus 18,
    Probelesodon 44, *Pteranodon* 40,
    Stegosaurus 27,
    Struthiomimus 19
fibula: *Archaeopteryx* 45,
    Diplodocus 15, *Iguanodon* 8,
    Protoceratops 37,
    Struthiomimus 19
fossils: endocast 28, 29,
    extracting 6-7, reading 8-9
fur 44, 45

G-H

gastroliths 31
hadrosaurs 10, 24, 28, 47
heart: *Anchisaurus* 14,
    Apatosaurus 32, 33,
    Archaeopteryx 45,
    Hylaeosaurus 22,
    Plesiosaurus 38, *Probelesodon* 44
Heterodontosaurus 11, 46
hips: *Apatosaurus* 32, 33,
    Deinonychus 20, *Diplodocus* 15,
    Euoplocephalus 17,
    Pachycephalosaurus 18,
    Plesiosaurus 39,
    Probelesodon 44, ,
    Protoceratops 37, *Pteranodon* 40,
    Spinosaurus 34, 35,
    Stegosaurus 27,
    Struthiomimus 19
humerus: *Apatosaurus* 33,
    Archaeopteryx 45, *Diplodocus* 15,
    Iguanodon 9, *Pteranodon* 41
Hylaeosaurus 22-23, 46
Hypsilophodon 47

I

ichthyosaurs 39
Ichthyosaurus 38
Iguanodon 8-9, 21
insects 42, 43
intestines: *Allosaurus* 30,
    Brachiosaurus 31,
    Diplodocus 15, *Hylaeosaurus* 22,
    Ichthyosaurus 39,
    Plesiosaurus 39, *Probelesodon* 44,
    Protoceratops 37, *Stegosaurus* 27

K-L

kidneys 31, 44
legs 14-15, 18-19
ligaments: *Deinonychus*, 20
    Diplodocus, 15,
    Mamenchisaurus 13

lungs: *Anchisaurus* 14,
    Apatosaurus 32, 33,
    Archaeopteryx 45, *Archelon* 39,
    Diplodocus 15,
    Hylaeosaurus 22,
    Plesiosaurus 38,
    Probelesodon 44, *Pteranodon* 40

M-N

Mamenchisaurus 13
Mantell, Gideon & Mary Ann 8
Meganeura 43
millipedes 42, 43
nasal passages 23, 24-25, 28

O

oesophagus: *Allosaurus* 30,
    Baryonyx 21, *Brachiosaurus* 30,
    Diplodocus 13,
    Parasaurolophus 24,
    Plesiosaurus 38,
    Probelesodon 45, *Pteranodon* 41
olfactory organ 23, 28, 29
ornithischian dinosaurs 46
Owen, Richard 22

P-Q

Pachycephalosaurus 17, 18-19, 47
Parasaurolophus 24, 47
phalanges 8, 18, 38
Plesiosaurus 38, 39
Probelesodon 44, 45
Protoceratops 36-37
Pteranodon 40
Pterodaustro 41
pterosaurs 40-41, 47
Quetzalcoatlus 41

R

radius 9, 21, 38, 41, 45
Rhoetosaurus 10
ribs: *Apatosaurus* 33,
    Archaeopteryx 45, *Archelon* 39,
    Brachiosaurus 31,
    Ceratosaurus 12, *Diplodocus* 15,
    Hylaeosaurus 23, *Iguanodon* 9,
    Pachycephalosaurus 18,
    Plesiosaurus 39, *Stegosaurus* 26

S

saurischian dinosaurs 46
sauropod dinosaurs 13, 28, 47
scapula 14, 26, 31
senses 28-29
skull: *Baryonyx* 21,
    Camarasaurus 28,
    Ceratosaurus 12,
    Corythosaurus 25,
    Diplodocus 13, *Iguanodon* 9,
    Pachycephalosaurus 19,
    Parasaurolophus 24,
    Probelesodon 45, *Pteranodon* 41,
    Rhoetosaurus 10,
    Struthiomimus 29,
    Tyrannosaurus 11
spinal cord 13, 26, 27
Spinosaurus 34-35
Stegosaurus 16, 26-27, 35, 46
Stenonychosaurus 26
stomach: *Allosaurus* 30,
    Anchisaurus 14,
    Archaeopteryx 45,

Brachiosaurus 31, centipede 42,
    cockroach 42, *Hylaeosaurus* 22,
    Ichthyosaurus 39, *Meganeura* 43,
    Probelesodon 44, *Stegosaurus* 27
Struthiomimus 29

T

tails 16-17, *Apatosaurus* 32,
    Archaeopteryx 44, 45,
    Archelon 39,
    Diplodocus 13, 16, 17,
    ichthyosaurs 39, *Iguanodon* 8,
    Mamenchisaurus 13,
    Pachycephalosaurus 17, 18,
    Plesiosaurus 39,
    Probelesodon 44,
    Spinosaurus 34,
    Stegosaurus 16, 27,
    Struthiomimus 19
teeth 10-11, *Allosaurus* 30,
    Anchisaurus 14,
    Archaeopteryx 44, *Baryonyx* 21,
    Brachiosaurus 30,
    Camarasaurus 28,
    Ceratosaurus 12 ,
    Deinonychus 21, *Diplodocus* 12,
    Euoplocephalus 16,
    Hypsilophodon 47,
    Ichthyosaurus 39, *Iguanodon* 8,
    Pachycephalosaurus 19,
    Plesiosaurus 38,
    Probelesodon 45,
    Protoceratops 36, pterosaurs 41,
    Stegosaurus 27, *Triceratops* 23
temperature control 26, 34-35
tibia: *Archaeopteryx* 45,
    Deinonychus 20, *Diplodocus* 15,
    Euoplocephalus 17,
    Iguanodon 8,
    Pachycephalosaurus 18,
    Protoceratops 37,
    Struthiomimus 19
trachea: *Apatosaurus* 33,
    arthropods 43, *Baryonyx* 21,
    Brachiosaurus 30,
    Camarasaurus 28, centipede 42,
    Diplodocus 13, *Hylaeosaurus* 23,
    Parasaurolophus 24,
    Plesiosaurus 38,
    Probelesodon 45, *Pteranodon* 41
Triceratops 6-7, 23, 36, 47
Tyrannosaurus 10, 11, 47

U – V – W

ulna: *Archaeopteryx* 45, *Baryonyx* 21,
    Deinonychus 21, *Diplodocus* 15,
    Iguanodon 9, *Plesiosaurus* 38,
    Pteranodon 41
vertebrae: *Allosaurus* 30,
    Archaeopteryx 45, *Archelon* 39,
    Baryonyx 21, *Ceratosaurus* 12,
    Diplodocus 13-17,
    Hylaeosaurus 23,
    Iguanodon 8, 9,
    Mamenchisaurus 13,
    Pachycephalosaurus 18, 19,
    Plesiosaurus 38,
    Probelesodon 44, 45,
    Protoceratops 37,
    Spinosaurus 34, 35,
    Stegosaurus 26
wings 40, 41, 43, 45

ACKNOWLEDGEMENTS

The illustrator and author would like to thank:
• The staff at the Zoological Society's Wolfson Library and the Natural History Museum, London, for their help and courtesy
• Sue Tunnicliff for her animal training

• Helen Cooper, who posed for the mini-dinos

Dorling Kindersley would like to thank: Miranda Smith for editorial help, Jane Parker for the index, and Neil Palfreyman for production guidance